William J. Fay

PAUL AND
HIS LETTERS

Proclamation Commentaries

PROCLAMATION COMMENTARIES

Second Edition
Revised and Enlarged

Gerhard Krodel, *Editor*

Leander E. Keck

FORTRESS PRESS   **PHILADELPHIA**

FIRST EDITION COPYRIGHT © 1979 BY FORTRESS PRESS
SECOND EDITION COPYRIGHT © 1988 BY FORTRESS PRESS

———————

Library of Congress Cataloging-in-Publication Data

Keck, Leander E.
Paul and his letters.

(Proclamation commentaries)
Bibliography: p.
Includes index.
1. Bible. N.T. Epistles of Paul—Theology.
2. Paul, the Apostle, Saint. I. Title. II. Series.
BS2651.K42 1988   225.9'24 [B]   88-7006
ISBN 0-8006-2340-1

———————

Printed in the United States of America   1-2340

To
Ernst Käsemann
with gratitude

CONTENTS

PREFACE TO THE
SECOND EDITION

Revising one's work elicits ambivalent feelings. On the one hand, I welcome the opportunity to improve, clarify, and occasionally modify what was written nearly a decade ago. On the other hand, I have sought to respect the integrity of the book by making only those changes that appear to be essential. To have interpolated new passages too frequently would have produced a book not unlike a colonial house to which a Victorian porch, a bay window here, and a picture window there have been added. Moreover, although the discussion of particular topics could easily have been expanded in order to account for the work of colleagues from whom I continue to learn, my overall understanding of Paul's thought has not changed drastically enough to warrant a complete recasting. To admit this, I know, is to make oneself vulnerable to the question that one Oxbridge don is reported to have put to another, "Are you dead, or merely revising?" Nonetheless, instead of engaging the steady flow of scholarly literature produced in the past decade, I have simply called attention to certain items to which the English-using reader will have ready access.

Although most reviewers have been generous in their positive assessment, two significant issues have been raised. The first concerns the structure of the discussion, the second pertains to its substance. Because I distinguish "The Gospel Paul Preached" from "What Paul Fought For," certain topics like ethics and faith/trust are discussed several times, and the basic theme of God's moral integrity (God's "righteousness") is dealt with at the end. While I have pondered this criticism repeatedly, it seemed best not to tamper with the structure, partly for the reasons stated in the foregoing paragraph, and partly because I continue to believe that the distinction is sound and fruitful. (To my knowledge, no one has deemed it wrong, and one reviewer called it a clear gain.) Once one approaches the task of presenting and interpreting Paul's thought with this distinction in mind, however, the alternatives are at least equally problematic. Either one takes up the polemical aspects of Paul's thought in each letter (and its alleged component parts of earlier letters) seriatim, or one discusses the thematic issues in a different sequence. The frustrating fact, of course, is that every attempt to present Paul's thought as a coherent whole disturbs the connections made in the occasion-oriented letters themselves, and scarcely avoids imposing a coherence that at various points and at various levels is probably foreign to the Apostle's mind. Yet if one forgoes reaching for coherence, one cannot bring Paul's thought into view but merely provides annotations to the letters. A major advance in our ability to order the presentation of Paul's thought in ways more akin to his own awaits a much fuller analysis of how the Apostle thought than is available at present. Even then it is unlikely that a flawless book on Paul and his thought can be written.

The substance of the presentation elicited two suggestive dissents of which I am aware, the one prompting me to clarify the construal of Paul's understanding of the law, the other to rethink the interpretation of Paul's understanding of faith/trust. If these criticisms prompted me to clarify and modify what I wrote before rather than retract it, this may reflect a decision to agree to disagree, rather than embodying the question a distinguished teacher used to ask, "Do you understand, or do you disagree?"

The most striking change is the inclusion of the Appendix, a brief survey of the study of Paul's theology. This material draws on a paper presented to the Society of Biblical Literature at its annual meeting in November 1986. This essay can be read independently of the rest of the book. Therefore some overlap between it and chapter 1 is unavoidable. Much to be desired is a more complete account, and assessment, of the scholarly effort to account for, understand, and interpret Paul's theology. To be desired even more is a book that sees historical criticism's treatment of Paul and early Christianity whole, and places it in the context of post-Enlightenment intellectual history (including its social and ecclesiastical factors). The scope of this Appendix, however, is much more modest. It will fulfill its purpose if it provides the reader with a sketch map of the terrain so that this book too can be seen in perspective.

LEANDER E. KECK
Christmas 1987

INTRODUCTION

Paul deserves to be discovered by those who do not know his letters and to be discovered afresh by those who do. He is not always easy to understand and often difficult to accept. Still, again and again readers have found him to have a word for the times.

No one can prescribe how Paul is to be discovered, or predict which facets of his thought will be most pertinent. One can, however, provide some help by making him more accessible, by sketching his message as a whole.

Paul's letters addressed particular issues in small house churches. Reading these letters is somewhat like overhearing a telephone conversation: one must always infer what is being said at the other end of the line, as well as the context of the conversation. Every critical introduction to the NT therefore places the individual letters into an inferred context. That sort of information will not be repeated. What interests us here is its import for our understanding of Paul and his letters as a whole.

The man and his message are not identical with the letters. Accordingly, the present volume is divided into three parts. Part I ("The Quest for the Historical Paul") takes note of major issues which have emerged in Pauline studies. Part II ("The Gospel Paul Preached") attempts to discern Paul's message apart from the controversies that evoked the letters. Paul was the bearer and interpreter of certain traditions, a particular form of early Christianity. Because most of his original readers had heard him before they read his letters, both he and they could assume a great deal in their conversation. Getting a sense of this common ground is the aim of Part II. "What Paul Fought For" (Part III) deals with fundamental themes which Paul asserted and defended in the letters. Naturally, the distinction between Part II and Part III is not exact. Even so, it situates Paul's theology between his background in early Christianity and his foreground in the crises of his churches. That is where the Paul we know theologized.

The letters of Paul are events in which Christian traditions were being interpreted into the lives and thoughts of real people. Today, Paul himself has become part of the Christian tradition. Nonetheless, he has the capacity to interact also with today's readers, who may be as surprised by him as those who read his letters first. That is what discovering Paul is all about. Even those who "know Paul" can discover him afresh.

PART I

THE QUEST FOR THE
HISTORICAL PAUL

Paul is surely the most influential figure of first-century Christianity. At the same time, he has been a divisive figure, repeatedly evoking both deep loyalty and fierce opposition. It is important at the outset to see why he has been, and continues to be, a problem.

The Paul of the New Testament is a composite, derived from the narrative about him and his mission in the Book of Acts, on the one hand, and from the thirteen letters that claim him as their author, on the other. The Paul of the letters, however, does not coincide completely with the Paul of Acts. If our knowledge of Paul depended entirely on Acts, for instance, we would not surmise that he had written letters, for it does not mention them nor does it describe the situations to which they were addressed; conversely, if we had only the letters, we could not speak of the "Damascus road" conversion, for Paul does not mention it either. Even if we rely only on the letters in order to understand his thought, we face serious problems because they are so diverse that there is reason to ask whether he himself wrote all of them.

Considerations like these imply that before turning to Paul himself, one should have a sense of the historical problems and a general orientation to the sources on which the ensuing discussion is based. Chapter 1 will therefore sketch the ways in which Paul is a problem, and chapter 2 will show why Paul's thought is not simply the sum of his thoughts in the genuine letters.

CHAPTER ONE

PAUL THE PROBLEM

Probably no other Christian has been hated so intensely as Paul. Even those who do not despise him may regret his influence on Christianity in the first place. They hold him responsible for displacing the religion of Jesus himself with a religion about Jesus, one represented by a church that preaches Jesus as a divine savior from sin, administers sacraments, and ordains clergy—none of which Jesus had inaugurated. A second group are the Jews. They blame Paul, the great apostate, for the fact that Christians have a distorted view of Judaism. Recently, however, a few Jewish scholars have found it possible to write appreciatively about Paul, while dissenting from him (e.g., Samuel Sandmel, *The Genius of Paul,* Richard L. Rubenstein, *My Brother Paul*). Those women who blame Paul for their second-class status in the church, and their inferior role in a culture shaped by it, are a third group alienated from Paul. To some extent, all three groups have misunderstood him. Perhaps seeing him in his historical context will alleviate some of the animus. But it is important to acknowledge at the outset that Paul is far from everybody's favorite Christian.

For those who admire Paul, he may be more of a problem than they realize. Can one be a sound representative of the gospel and seldom quote Jesus? How valid an interpreter of Christianity is Paul? The more apparent it becomes that Paul's theology is not interchangeable with that of John (Robin Scroggs sees deeper continuities as well as major differences between them; *Christology in Paul and John*), the clearer it is that Paul does not speak for the whole NT. Indeed, does he speak for anyone but himself? If one stands with Paul, does one stand with a loner, with one who could write that there is no valid gospel other than his, even if an angel were to preach it (Gal. 1:8)? Does an adequate view of Christianity require us to supplement Paul, to round off his sharp edges and to domesticate him into the mainstream? Many have thought so.

Seeing Paul historically will not solve all problems readers have had with him, or might discover in him, but it is one way of getting some perspective. Consequently, this chapter will sketch three historical aspects of the problem of Paul.

The Problem of Paul in the New Testament

First, Paul presents a problem within the NT because he dominates it. Of the 657 pages of Greek text (Nestle-Aland, 26th ed.), 156 claim to come from Paul. If we add the 24 pages of the Letter to the Hebrews, which got into the canon because the church in Egypt believed Paul wrote it, more than one-fourth of the NT is associated with a man who had not been a disciple of Jesus, whereas Peter, the leading figure in the circle around Jesus, is represented by only fourteen pages. In addition, more than half of the Book of Acts is devoted to Paul. Did Paul dominate Christianity in his own time as much as he now dominates the NT? Or does Paul's place in the canon make him loom larger than he actually was?

Second, Paul appears as a problem in the NT because the letters from the man often do not support the report about him in Acts. Because the Paul of Acts is the Paul most people know best, one should guard against assimilating the Paul of the letters to the Paul of Acts. The Paul of the letters must determine our understanding of the man and his thoughts. Acts is a secondary source for historical inquiry; the first-hand sources are the letters. Nonetheless, Acts remains the only account of Paul's career that we have from the first centuries, and no study of Paul can ignore it completely. (See *Acts* by Gerhard Krodel in Proclamation Commentaries.)

The letters themselves constitute the third way in which Paul is a problem in the NT, for there are such fundamental differences among them that most scholars are convinced that some cannot have come from Paul. There is virtual unanimity that the following letters are authentic: Romans, 1, 2 Corinthians, Galatians, Philippians, 1 Thessalonians, Philemon. But there is almost equal agreement that the Pastorals (1, 2 Timothy, Titus) are not genuine. The majority of students regard Ephesians to be nongenuine as well, but opinion is divided over Colossians and 2 Thessalonians. (For a traditional view of authorship of what here is regarded as deutero-Pauline, see Luke T. Johnson, *The Writings of the New Testament.*)

For our purposes, it is more important to see the consequences of regarding only the seven letters as genuine than it is to justify not expanding the list. First of all, if the seven letters are genuine, any interpretation of Paul restricting itself to them rests on a solid base. The more one relies on what is said only in Ephesians or 2 Thessalonians, for instance, the less secure is the interpretation of Paul. In no case should a disputed letter be the basis for interpreting something in a genuine letter. For example, Col. 3:1 speaks of the believer as already having been raised with Christ; this must not guide the interpretation of Rom. 6:5, where Paul writes that participation in Christ's resurrection is a future event.

Moreover, the distinctive emphasis of each deutero-Pauline letter is so pronounced that including them in a discussion of Paul himself shifts the center of gravity. This is especially true of Ephesians, in which the church is the central theme. Not surprisingly, those interpretations of Paul that emphasize his ecclesiology rely on Ephesians, and read the theology of the genuine letters through the lens of this deutero-Pauline one.

Further, if it is indeed the case, as I think likely, that Philippians and Philemon were written from Ephesus, then all seven letters were written in the 50s. This chronological conclusion has important implications: (*a*) The earliest letter is 1 Thessalonians and Romans is the latest. Behind Romans, the most mature statement of Paul's theology, lie the controversies worked through in previous letter writing. (*b*) The closer the letters stand to one another in time, the less persuasive are efforts to trace development in Paul's thought. Differences within the genuine letters must be accounted for on a basis other than development in Paul's thinking. (*c*) Our letters come from but a slice of Paul's career. From the fifteen years between his conversion and 1 Thessalonians we have nothing except reports in Acts. Similarly, we have nothing from the last decade when he was a prisoner in Palestine and in Rome except reports in Acts.

In other words, whoever wants to read the undisputed letters of Paul must extract this genuine corpus from the order in which the NT now has them:

Romans
1 Corinthians
2 Corinthians
Galatians
[Ephesians]
Philippians
[Colossians]
1 Thessalonians
[2 Thessalonians]

[1 Timothy]
[2 Timothy]
[Titus]
Philemon

Moreover, whoever wants to read the seven undisputed letters in the order in which Paul wrote them must rearrange the sequence. This effort, however, is complicated by the likelihood that a number of the genuine letters actually combine two or more letters from Paul (see chap. 2). Given the subtlety of the evidence, it is not surprising that scholars have not been able to produce a widely accepted list of all of Paul's correspondence in chronological order. This too frustrates efforts to talk convincingly about the "development" of Paul's thought.

Finally, the consequences we have noted are all historical, not theological. That is, they concern attempts to understand Paul himself in his own context, not with the theological validity of the deutero-Pauline letters, nor with their authority in the canon. What Ephesians says about the church may or may not be valid, irrespective of whether or not Paul wrote it. The interpreter of the NT needs to be clear on this point, lest historical conclusions and hypotheses prejudge theological issues improperly. (See Leander E. Keck and Victor Paul Furnish, *The Pauline Letters*.)

To conclude, "the message of Paul" is not self-evident because there are different "Pauls" in the NT. Indeed, the latest book in the NT points out that the church was having trouble understanding him properly:

> And count the forbearance of our Lord as salvation. So also our beloved brother Paul wrote to you according to the wisdom given him, speaking of this as he does in all his letters. There are some things in them hard to understand, which the ignorant and unstable twist to their own destruction, as they do the other scriptures. (2 Pet. 3:15–16)

Also in the ancient church Paul was a problem.

Paul the Problem in Early Christianity

To understand better Paul's place in early Christianity, it is necessary to see that the NT itself incorporates alternative interpretations of the gospel. Paul does not speak for everyone. It is useful to recognize several of the types of Christianity that were developing in the first century.

To begin with, the Christianity that developed in Jerusalem differed markedly from Paul's. The modern study of Paul began in the 1830s when

F. C. Baur contended that the whole apostolic period was dominated by a tension between Jewish Christianity led by Peter and a gentile Christianity represented by Paul. In one way or another, this theory has persisted, even though today it is not Peter but James, Jesus' brother, who is credited with leading a Christianized Judaism in Jerusalem. James's Christianity (not to be associated with the Epistle of James, written by someone else) insisted on observing the Jewish law (Acts 21:18–20). We see this also in the tradition quoted by the fourth-century historian, Eusebius, concerning James: he was a very devout Jew, praying so often in the temple that he got calluses on his knees like a camel. Baur and his successors may have exaggerated certain aspects of the tension between Paul and James, and Johannes Munck (*Paul and the Salvation of Mankind*) may have underestimated it, but there is no doubt that the differences were deep.

Another type of Christianity differed from that of both James and Paul, namely, the Johannine. Adolf Deissmann (*Paul,* 7) was wrong in calling John Paul's greatest interpreter, for John does not develop Pauline Christianity but represents another alternative to it. Rudolf Bultmann (*Theology of the New Testament,* 2:7–10) rightly saw that themes important to Paul are absent from John (e.g., the problem of the law). Conversely, what is important to John is not found in Paul (e.g., the Paraclete [the Spirit] as the interpreter of the Jesus tradition).

There was also outright opposition to Paul, both in his own time and afterward. As we shall see, Paul had to contend with the opposition even in his own churches, especially in Galatia and Corinth. Traveling preachers appeared in Corinth after he had left and undermined his work there so seriously that he said they were "false apostles, deceitful workmen, disguising themselves as apostles of Christ" (2 Cor. 11:13). Similarly, he was so irritated at those who opposed his gospel in Galatia by demanding that gentile Christians circumcise themselves, that he wished the knife would slip during the operation (Gal. 5:12). Long afterward, in the second century, the Ebionites (Jewish Christians who called themselves "the Poor" and claimed to be the descendants from the original church) hated Paul as the arch-heretic.

Finally, the friends of Paul struggled not only against his enemies but to some extent also with each other for the rights to Paul's legacy (as 2 Peter saw). Acts aims to present a normative account of Paul, portraying him as acknowledged by the Jerusalem church. The insistence that Paul was in good standing with the Jerusalem church shows that it was necessary to defend Paul and his successors from the charge of being "Paulinists"—a sectarian movement. Moreover, Acts shows Paul to be as loyal a Jew as he could have been under the circumstances. He circumcised Timothy even though it was not necessary theologically (Acts 16:1–3). Paul was eager to observe the Jewish festival of Pentecost in Jerusalem, like a pilgrim (Acts 20:16). Once there, he agreed to James's strategy for showing that he was faithful to Judaism (Acts 21:17–26). Before the Sanhedrin, Acts has Paul claim he is (not "was") a Pharisee, whose advocacy of the resurrection doctrine succeeded in dividing the court (Acts 23:1–10). Apparently Acts is defending Paul, and thereby the Christians who look to him, from the charge of being a renegade Jew. This may well have been a problem in Luke's generation, which needed to know who Paul really was.

Some friends of Paul also produced letters in his name and each document pulls Paul in a different direction. Ephesians emphasizes ecclesiology. The Pastorals present him as the advocate of a highly institutionalized church. On the other hand, 2 Thessalonians makes Paul combat another (now lost) spurious letter circulating in his name (2 Thess. 2:2), and has him advocate an outright apocalyptic teaching. The spurious letter attacked by 2 Thessalonians advocated a position similar to that opposed by 2 Timothy—that the Day of the Lord had already come (2 Tim. 2:16–18). This is the sign of a gnostic interpretation of Paul. Recently, Elaine Pagels analyzed the ways second-century Valentinian gnostics interpreted Paul along Valentinian lines (*The Gnostic Paul*). Later still, the apocryphal correspondence between Paul and Seneca portrayed Paul in somewhat Stoicized terms. Still later, the Acts of Paul had him advocate Christian asceticism. Indeed, Dennis R. MacDonald has argued that the Acts of Paul (late second century) contain earlier legends which portray the apostle as a social radical, and that the Pastoral Epistles were written against these same earlier legends.

The most ardent friend of Paul in the early second century was Marcion. He concluded that after Paul's death his Judaizing opponents not only prevailed and Judaized Christianity but tampered with his letters in order to make Paul speak favorably of the OT and of the Creator. In the name of Paul, Marcion became the first reformer, and he split many churches. He decided that Paul's gospel had been the Gospel of Luke (also corrupted by the Judaizers). To restore true Christianity, he purged the letters of Paul and the Gospel of Luke of the pro–OT parts and so provided his churches with the first distinctly Christian canon—the Gospel of Luke and the Letters of Paul (minus the Pastorals). A major achievement of Irenaeus and Tertullian was to reclaim Paul from some of his most ardent friends, the gnostics and Marcion, by showing that Paul's real friends were in the emerging catholic church. The catholicity of the church manifests itself in the fact that the NT includes epistles attributed to apostles besides Paul (Peter, John, James, Jude), and Gospels besides Luke.

Enough of this fascinating story has been sketched to show that Paul was a controversial figure in early Christianity. The Christians of the early centuries too wrestled with the problem: Who was Paul really and what did he really teach? In modern times, the controversies have resumed.

The Problem of Paul in
Critical Scholarship

During the past century and a half, historical-critical scholarship has attempted to understand Paul—the man, his work, his thought—as a historical phenomenon of his own time and place. In doing so, it has discovered a set of interlocking problems and debated a variety of proposals for solving them. A brief account of these efforts can be found in the Appendix. Here it will suffice to identify two types of problems fundamental to a historical understanding of Paul: (1) The first concerns the dominant cultural-religious influence upon him and his thought. Is he to be understood primarily in light of Hellenistic religiosity or in light of Judaism? Or is this a false alternative? (2) The second concerns the phenomenon of the Pauline mission in antiquity: How did Paul go about the task of propagating Christianity and nurturing the small house churches that he created?

Attempts to understand Paul primarily in terms of Hellenism tend to emphasize either his view of the sacraments or his Christology. The former calls attention to the theme of participating in Christ's death through baptism and the Lord's Supper, the latter to his view of Christ as the divine being who descended to earth where he achieved salvation and then was exalted to God's right hand after his death.

Paul's view of the sacraments has sometimes been seen to reflect those Hellenistic mystery cults in which the initiate appropriated the divine life/death of the deity, and so was reborn. According to this view, the almost "magical" power of baptism manifests itself in the casual way in which Paul mentions the baptism for the dead (1 Cor. 15:29). So potent is the sacramental eating of the Lord's body that those who ate "unworthily" became ill and some died (1 Cor. 11:29-30). Such passages, often bypassed by readers, are said to be tips of the icebergs, revealing that Paul owes far more to the mystery cults than appears on the surface. Since there is no Jewish precedent for such ideas as participating in the deity's death (Rom. 6:5), it must be from the cults that Paul derived them.

It remains, however, that there are formidable obstacles to reading Paul in this light. For one thing, he never uses the term "rebirth" nor does he appear to have made baptismal initiation central to his work (1 Cor. 1:14–17, see chap. 4). Moreover, the reference to baptism for the dead is too obscure to become the basis of interpretation. Above all, although the cults were ancient already in Paul's time, it is not clear that they were a major factor on the scene in his day. Rather they seem to have become more prominent only later. The attempts to interpret Paul in light of the mystery cults did, however, call attention to the "realism" of Paul's language about participation in Christ's death and signaled the need to be wary of taking such language to be "merely symbolic"—a way of talking that neither Paul nor anyone else in his time would have understood.

The Hellenistic interpretation of Paul has emphasized also his indebtedness to the myth of the descending/ascending redeemer, especially as this has been found in Gnosticism. Sometimes this is connected with the myth of the Primal Man, Anthropos, which has been traced far back into antiquity. In 1 Cor. 15:45–49 Paul speaks of the "man from heaven" who is to embody human destiny in contrast with Adam, the "man of dust" who constitutes human fate. Sometimes this myth of the redeemer, who himself was redeemed from human existence which he assumed, is found behind Phil. 2:5–11, which celebrates the humiliation/exaltation of God's Son, or behind 1 Cor. 2:8, which speaks of the incognito appearing of the Son on earth, who has slipped by the invisible powers that dominate the globe (see chap. 5). This myth is intimately bound up with the gnostic view of redemption, which will concern us in chapter 7. It is also linked with the idea that the saved constitute a "body" whose "head" is the redeemer—a view found in Col. 1:18 and Eph. 4:15–16, and which may lie behind 1 Cor. 12:27 (which does not mention the "head"). Moreover, in 1 Corinthians 2—3 Paul appears to reason like a gnostic who claims that as a Spirit-person, he can know what no one else can know.

Many students have serious problems with any interpretation of Paul which relies on texts later than Paul to reconstruct backgrounds that influenced him. This is the case for the alleged gnostic influence on Paul's Christology. This objection can be overemphasized easily and made into a false refuge, because the later texts (the only ones available) clearly contain ideas that were much older and that do illumine Paul's assertions. More important, it has been shown that the redeemed redeemer myth is largely a composite made by modern scholars who drew a variety of material together, and that in Paul's day there was no single dominant redeemer myth. Nonetheless, the many myths do fall into a certain pattern, and the pattern was probably taken for granted by Paul and his readers. In other words, there is more reason to associate Paul's Christology with Hellenistic mythology than there is to derive his view of the sacraments from mystery cults.

Attempts to understand Paul primarily in terms of Judaism tend to emphasize one of three types of Judaism: Hellenistic, Rabbinic, or apocalyptic. That Paul was a Hellenized Jew is evident not only by his mastery of the Septuagint (the translation of the synagogue Bible into Greek, made several centuries before), but also by his competent use of Greek rhetorical forms (see chap. 2). Furthermore, in 1 Cor. 1:24 he calls Christ the wisdom of God, a standard motif of Hellenized Judaism. Similarly, Rom. 1:18–32 echoes Hellenistic Jewish attitudes toward Gentiles.

That Paul was trained in Pharisaic Judaism in Jerusalem is reported in Acts 22:3. Moreover, although Paul himself never refers to his studying with Gamaliel in Jerusalem, he does refer to his pre-Christian life as a Pharisee (Phil. 3:4–5) and to his previous zeal for the traditions of his fathers (Gal. 1:14). He not only uses the technical rabbinic vocabulary for receiving and transmitting traditions (1 Cor. 15:3) but also argues from Scripture in rabbinic ways and relies on traditions developed among the rabbis (1 Cor. 10:1–5). Above all, Paul's concern to relate Christ to the law of Moses—the central theme of Pharisaism—manifests the abiding influence of this aspect of Judaism upon him. As we shall see, it is *what* Paul says about the law that causes some scholars to conclude that he misrepresented Pharisaism.

Paul was deeply affected by another strand of Judaism as well—apocalyptic. Admittedly, this is more difficult to delineate because some of the ideas and motifs commonly associated with apocalyptic thought were held also by the Pharisees and their successors, the rabbis (e.g., the wrath of God, the coming judgment, and the resurrection of the dead). More important, Paul did not simply share a set of ideas with apocalyptic; at certain points the apocalyptic outlook provided the framework for his thought as a whole (e.g., the view that over against the glorious future all of history is regarded as "this age" [Gal. 1:4], which is now passing away [1 Cor. 7:31, where kosmos = aiōn]). Indeed J. Christiaan Beker (*Paul the Apostle*) contends that the eschatological triumph of God in Christ, understood in apocalyptic terms, constitutes the heart of Paul's gospel. At the same time, Paul did not simply insert the gospel meaning of Jesus into an inherited apocalyptic world view. Nor could he, because the driving question of apocalyptic theology—the innocent suffering of the righteous—was for him transformed by Jesus' cross and resurrection (Leander E. Keck, "Paul and Apocalyptic Theology," *Interpretation* 38 [1984] 229–41). The perceptive reader will therefore discern both Paul's use of apocalyptic ideas and his transformation of apocalyptic perspectives.

The interesting thing about these attempts to locate the dominant influence on Paul is that while no one of them succeeds in accounting for Paul, all of them have seen something that is really there. In other words, Paul was influenced by all these factors, some more than others. Exactly how they fit together logically will probably continue to elude students of Paul. The point is that he lived in a syncretistic era. It would be surprising if he did not represent something of an amalgam himself.

Several things need to be borne in mind for the interpretation of such a figure for religious and theological ends. (*a*) The origin of this idea or that motif is of interest to the historian trying to locate Paul in his own culture, but it was of no interest to Paul himself. Had anyone pointed out to him the "parallels" to his ideas and phrases, he may well have responded with imperial indifference. Adequate treatment of "parallels" and "influences" requires thorough knowledge of both Paul's cultural context and his letters, lest one overemphasize either his dependence or his originality. Even when parallels to Paul's ideas and practices can be documented, it is not always evident whether he adopted them as part of a deliberate missionary strategy or whether he simply followed convention. Indeed, we shall see that he could appropriate the language of his readers in order to argue against them on their own turf. Nor should one overlook the possibility of "negative influences"—Paul's (deliberate?) avoidance of certain ideas, terms, and practices common in his day. Above all, one should remember Paul's capacity to adapt for his own ends whatever he shared with his environment. (*b*) Our labels tend to get in the way. Far too often it is assumed that if one of Paul's phrases sounds gnostic it could not at the same time be derived from Hellenized Judaism, that what has been identified as rabbinic should not be found among apocalyptists. Labels like gnostic, Hellenistic

Jewish, Stoic, apocalyptic, do not mark off fixed boundaries but merely identify the range within which one seeks family resemblances of ideas. In antiquity ideas did not flow in pipes. (*c*) The religious and theological validity of Paul's ideas in no way depends on how one judges their antecedents and parallels in antiquity. An idea does not necessarily become more significant or adequate when one can show that it was more at home in Judaism than in Hellenism, though some discussions imply that ideas are valid only if they have been circumcised.

Actually, the question of "backgrounds" and "influences" cannot be restricted to Paul but must include his readers as well. Paul's letters reflect the interaction, and sometimes the collision, of somewhat diverse backgrounds and influences which met in the newly formed, small Christian groups to which the letters were sent. Before looking at the letters themselves, it is useful to note briefly the character of these groups and their place in the Greco-Roman world.

Paul concentrated his efforts in the major cities of Anatolia (Turkey) and the Aegean basin, cosmopolitan centers of trade and travel. Here he formed groups of Christians consisting of both Gentiles and Hellenized Jews, the former being the clear majority. Some of these Gentiles converted directly from polytheism (Gal. 4:8; 1 Thess. 1:9–10), while others had previously been affiliated loosely with the synagogue, the "God-fearers" (Acts 13:26). These converts were not drawn primarily from the "lower classes," the dispossessed and the destitute, as has been claimed, but from the artisans and merchants, in whose apartments above the workshops and shops they assembled—parents and children, relatives, employees, and slaves. Paul himself worked as a tentmaker—because this provided a point of contact (Acts 18:1–4), prevented him from becoming a burden on his congregation (1 Thess. 2:9), and distinguished him from those itinerant teachers who charged fees and often took advantage of their followers (see Ronald F. Hock, *The Social Context of Paul's Ministry: Tentmaking and Apostleship*).

However great may have been the Jewish influence on Paul's thought, his practice was in most ways typically Hellenistic, as Abraham J. Malherbe's study of Paul's mission in Macedonia has shown (*Paul and the Thessalonians*). In a day when popular philosophy summoned people to moral conversion, whether to Stoic rationality or to Epicurean serenity, itinerant philosophers too formed their converts into groups where they found mutual support and received ongoing instruction. The similarities, as well as the differences, between Paul's pastoral methods and vocabulary and those of his contemporary moralists is often striking. At the same time, given a polytheistic culture in which people often acknowledged several gods and could be initiated into more than one mystery religion, and given a society in which one could belong to many clubs and associations simultaneously, one feature distinguished Paul's groups—their exclusiveness, based on inherited Jewish monotheism and the conviction that only Jesus is Lord.

Paul's congregations, moreover, understood themselves to be part of a network, the church (*ekklesia*), which was the beachhead of the New Age. This distinct sense of identity entailed making a number of adjustments in their style of life (see chap. 7). Further, they experienced a spiritual energy, understood as the power of the Holy Spirit, which expressed itself in diverse ways, including ecstasy and miracle working (Rom. 15:19; 2 Cor. 12:12). Understandably, these fledgling congregations, drawn from all sorts of backgrounds, were easily divided over all sorts of issues, especially after Paul had moved on to the next city. (In *The First Urban Christians*, Wayne A. Meeks explores such matters in detail, drawing upon sociological categories.) Were it not for these problems, Paul would not have become the letter writer we know.

CHAPTER TWO

THE THEOLOGY OF PAUL AND THE THEOLOGY OF THE LETTERS

It is a commonplace to say that it is easier to interpret Paul than Jesus because we have direct access to Paul's own letters but only indirect access to Jesus through the Gospels. Even so, the theology of Paul and the theology expressed in the letters are not identical. This is not because Paul thought one thing and wrote another. Rather, this distinction results from the character of Paul's letters as we know them. What we know of Paul's theology depends on *the letters we have;* yet the letters themselves were significantly affected not only by what lay *ahead* of them (among the readers) but also by what lay *behind* them (in the writer and his resources). Each of these will be explored in this chapter.

The Character of Paul's Letters

1. The first thing to see is that Paul's letters come to us as a collection made and accepted by the church as "The Letters of Paul." Today scholarly judgment has distinguished genuine from nongenuine letters within this collection (see chap. 1), but the collection itself represents the ancient church's attempt to do the same thing, for the church excluded the Letter to the Laodiceans, so-called 3 Corinthians, and the exchange of brief letters between Paul and the philosopher Seneca. In other words, the concern to identify which letters claiming to be from Paul are genuine and which are secondary is as old as the canon. The author of 2 Thessalonians had to warn the readers about another "Pauline" letter claiming that Paul taught that the Day of the Lord had already come (2 Thess. 2:2; a similar point was combated in 2 Tim. 2:16–18). When modern critical judgment concludes that 2 Thessalonians itself is nongenuine, it is simply extending and refining the process that began even before the original collection was formed.

The Pauline collection not only includes more than Paul himself wrote but also less than everything he produced. We know of letters that have disappeared. In 1 Cor. 5:9 Paul refers to a letter which was misunderstood, as least in part, and which Paul now explains. The theory that part of this letter is now embedded in 2 Corinthians, at 6:14—7:1, has not persuaded all students. Further, 2 Cor. 2:4 mentions a letter written with intense anguish. Part of it appears to be included in 2 Corinthians (chaps. 10-13), but part of it also appears to be lost. Colossians 4:16 refers to a letter "from Laodicea," evidently one that will come from there to Colossae. Even if Paul did not write Colossians, a matter of continuing dispute, there is no reason to doubt that there once circulated a letter to the Laodiceans. (The brief "Letter to the Laodiceans" which we do have is certainly a different work, for it is merely a pastiche of Pauline phrases.)

More important, Paul's letters were also edited. Of the seven undoubtedly genuine letters, only in the case of Philemon can we be certain that what we have is virtually identical with what Paul wrote. In a few cases, the manuscripts reveal this editorial work. For example, the concluding benediction of Romans appears at 16:25-27 in most manuscripts, but P[46] has it after 15:33, some after 14:23, some at both places, and others omit it altogether. Evidently different editions were prepared for church use.

Usually, however, the evidence for editorial work is internal, not disclosed by manuscript differences. For instance, Phil. 1:1 mentions bishops and deacons. Since it appears that our Philippians is a compilation of shorter letters, one suspects that here the editor has updated the greeting to include church officials. Apart from this reference, there is no indication that such offices existed during Paul's own time.

The most common evidence for editing is tension in content or difficult transitions from one part to another. A few examples will illustrate both:

(a) Where the transitions from one paragraph to another are inexplicably abrupt, it is almost certain that here an editor juxtaposed parts of two letters. For instance, at Phil. 3:1 (and in the foregoing lines) Paul strikes a note of joy, but at 3:2 the text shifts to a bitter warning: "Look out for the dogs, look out for the evil-workers," and so forth. This tone continues through the rest of chapter 3, but at 4:1 the theme of joy returns. In other words, 3:2-21 is part of another letter. Our 2 Corinthians is also widely regarded as composite. We already noted that 2 Cor. 6:14—7:1 is part of another letter. To test this judgment, one has only to read 7:2 after 6:13 to see that without the intervening material the text reads smoothly and reasons coherently.

(b) Sometimes the tensions between parts of a present letter are not so clearly related to abrupt transitions, but nonetheless suggest, to some students at least, that an editor has been rather skillful in joining parts of diverse letters. One example is 2 Corinthians 8 and 9, both of which deal with the collection of funds for Jerusalem, but from different points of view (see Hans Dieter Betz, *Second Corinthians 8 and 9*). A less obvious instance is 1 Corinthians 8—10, where some students see parts of different letters because in chapter 8 Paul argues that since idols have no existence, food that had been offered to them in a token ritual may be eaten by Christians unless doing so offends a "weak" brother. In chapter 10, he seems to argue that because pagan sacrifice is actually offered to demons, Christians cannot participate in cult meals of both the pagan shrines and the church. On the other hand, many interpreters see only a refinement of the argument in chapter 8, not evidence that chapter 10 is a later, different letter fragment.

Given the nature of the evidence and the role of personal judgment about what is too different to have been written in the same letter, it is inevitable that proposals to factor 1 and 2 Corinthians and Philippians into component parts have differed considerably among themselves. Some more cautious students of Paul have therefore concluded that such proposals cancel one another and have refused to grant that these letters are composite. But neither the fallibility of a given reconstruction nor the diversity of proposals disallows the main point—that at least 2 Corinthians and Philippians are compiled. The point is that what we have are those forms of Paul's letters that were prepared for church use long after Paul himself wrote them.

(*c*) Another phenomenon appears from time to time in these letters—the addition of brief statements, sometimes phrases, to the text. These are of two kinds, interpolations (new material) and glosses (interpretive comments originally made in the margin, then incorporated by a copyist). It is not always possible to differentiate precisely what is gloss and what is interpolation, but many of these brief post-Pauline additions have been detected (see William O. Walker, Jr., "The Burden of Proof in Identifying Interpolations in the Pauline Letters," *New Testament Studies* 33 [1987], 610–18). Because good manuscripts often include them, the additions were made very early. Several of these interpolations have been rather influential, unfortunately. One is 1 Thess. 2:14–16, where the text regards the fall of Jerusalem (the probable referent) as God's punishment on the Jews for killing Jesus and persecuting Christians. Another is 1 Cor. 14:33b–36, which forbids women to speak in church worship. Not only does this contradict 1 Cor. 11:5, which assumes that women do pray and prophesy in church, but it also agrees with the post-Pauline author of 1 Tim. 2:11–12. So Paul has been blamed for a view that he did not have.

We may summarize: (a) we do not have access to Paul's letters as he wrote them, but only to the letters as they were incorporated into a collection; (b) several of our letters combine parts of different letters, written on different occasions but presumably to the same readers; (c) secondary materials were added here and there, and some parts of letters omitted. The conclusion is clear: the letters of Paul as we have them cannot be simply equated with what Paul himself wrote. What the letters present us with is Paul as he was transmitted by the church. This is one reason why the theology of the letters is not simply identical with the theology of Paul himself.

(2.) Second, we see that Paul wrote letters that were occasional— occasioned by particular circumstances in his churches. None of his letters was written simply as a means of self-expression and then shared with friends, the way some persons write poetry as a hobby. Nor were the letters written for the general public, as if produced for publication and sale to a "religious market." Rather, they were written for particular congregations (small house churches) who had particular problems. (To some extent Romans is an exception because Paul had not yet been to Rome (see Karl P. Donfried, *The Romans Debate*). The particularity of each occasion accounts for the diversity among the letters.

Several aspects of the occasional character of Paul's letters deserve mention. (a) Because the letters are Paul's responses to what was going on among the readers, it is necesary to understand the situation to which the letters respond. (b) All we can know of the situation, however, must be inferred from the answer; we have no independent, non-Pauline, access to the situation. After inferring the question we can interpret the answer. There is no alternative to such circular reasoning. (c) One must assume that Paul did not misunderstand or misrepresent the situation. This point has been challenged by Walter Schmithals, who contended that, at least to begin with, Paul misunderstood the problem in Corinth, with the result that his answer in 1 Corinthians 15 was partly misplaced (*Gnosticism in Corinth*, e.g., 155–6). But Paul was much closer to the Corinthians than is Schmithals, or any other modern. (d) Paul's understanding of the issues did not necessarily coincide with what the readers themselves thought. The Galatians, for instance, thought that accepting circumcision would make them first-class Christians, but Paul thought it would nullify the Christian faith altogether. (e) Even if we were to "add up" all the letters, they would not contain everything that Paul believed or thought. Rather, the result would be a compend of things Paul deemed necessary to say to a spectrum of issues. Because Paul addressed "pressure points" in his churches, he needed only to mention other matters which he did not regard as problematic. What was not in dispute could be assumed, such as using the Bible of the synagogue as Scripture also for the church.

The occasional character of Paul's letters calls for a measure of sensitivity on the part of the interpreter. To interpret them calls for more than making their contents intelligible. One needs to make Paul's point in a manner that confronts today's readers in a way analogous to what occurred originally. To facilitate this, the interpreter needs to penetrate not only Paul's "answers" but also the "question" until what becomes apparent is the extent to which today's readers share the same problem as the original ones. The greater the similarity, the more directly Paul's response may address also our own. For example, if today "tongue speaking" disrupts a congregation and leads to a certain pride on the part of those who have this capacity, then Paul's word in 1 Corinthians 12—14 can be as pertinent today as then. If the interpreter first finds the particularity of the original occasions to be an obstacle to appropriating Paul, it is probably because one expects the letters to articulate timeless truths and principles to be applied, rather than timely words to concrete situations which are prototypes of our own. In other words, in the long run it is precisely the particularity of the occasions that makes Paul's letters perennially significant.

3. The third characteristic of Paul's letters concerns their formal elements, what one might call their components, and their mode of argument. It has long been recognized that Paul's letters both adopt and adapt the letter-writing conventions of the time. The Greek letter had three elements: an introductory statement (name of sender and recipient, greetings, a word of thanks to the gods, and sometimes a wish that the gods aid the recipient); the body of the letter containing the subject matter to be communicated; and the conclusion (final greetings to mutual acquaintances, closing prayer-wish to the gods, sometimes the date). In recent years, scholars have studied intensively the formal elements (stereotyped phrases, conventions of moving from one part to another, etc.) and types of letters (letters of recommendation, personal correspondence, official letters, etc.), drawing especially on a mass of letters written on papyrus. William Doty's *Letters in Primitive Christianity* provides an excellent overview of the results. The

recent books by Stanley K. Stowers (*Letter Writing in Greco-Roman Antiquity*) and John L. White (*Light from Ancient Letters*) analyze various kinds of letters and provide abundant examples in translation. (White also provides the Greek texts.) By analyzing Greco-Roman letters (Greek, Latin, Hebrew, Aramaic) we understand Paul's letter writing better.

a) First of all, we understand that Paul's letters were not dashed off spontaneously, nor were they private correspondence. The first great student of the papyri letters, Adolf Deissmann, argued for both of these points, but wrongly. Deissmann, moreover, distinguished too sharply the letter (personal, spontaneous, informal correspondence) from the epistle, a self-conscious literary production designed for publication. Paul's letters actually combine features of both. They embody Paul's intense personal involvement in the issues but they were also designed to be read (aloud) in the congregations (1 Thess. 5:27; Philemon 2). Paul apparently wrote these letters when he could not personally visit the congregations. He regarded his letters as "stand-ins" for his own presence. When a letter from Paul was read, it was as though Paul himself were speaking. Moreover, Paul clearly wrote out of his sense of apostolic authority. Paul did not see himself expressing merely personal opinions and preferences, but as articulating the normative meaning of the revelation of God in Jesus Christ. The letter to Philemon shows how Paul could write short personal letters, though v. 2 implies that he also expected it to be shared with the church.

b) Second, we have learned that Paul carefully structured his letters, and modified letter-writing conventions at certain points:

(1) *(a)* The standard greeting (A to B, Greetings!) becomes more elaborate. Except in the case of Romans and Galatians, Paul mentions associates. Moreover, he states his apostolic authorization (1 and 2 Corinthians; Galatians) when that is a factor in the situation being addressed; otherwise he characterizes himself as a slave of Christ (Philippians) or as a prisoner (Philemon). In Romans he combines these modes of self-introduction: "Paul, a slave of Christ Jesus, a called apostle" and then elaborates, "set apart for the gospel of God." The Galatian situation prompted him to defend his apostleship in the first line, "not from men nor through man but through Jesus Christ and God the Father. . . ." Thus Paul's modifications of the greetings alert the reader to the content to follow. The concluding element of the Greek greeting (*chairein* = "Greeting") Paul modified to grace (*charis*) and peace, the latter reflecting the Jewish *shalōm*.

(2) *(b)* In place of a phrase thanking the gods for his own good health, Paul

developed a distinctive paragraph of thanksgiving (found in all his letters except Galatians because the crisis was so severe that Paul could not give thanks) in which he expressed gratitude for the vitality of the Christian faith among the readers. Moreover, the thanksgiving paragraph often modulates into an eschatological chord. Thereby Paul reminded the readers that salvation would be completed at the Parousia (the coming of Christ). Furthermore, the thanksgiving subtly announces themes to be developed in the body of the letter. Thus Rom. 1:11–12 tactfully speaks of Paul's desire to share a spiritual gift with the Romans, and the following verses (13–17) show that what he wants to share is his understanding of the gospel, whose formulation climaxes the whole paragraph and so announces the theme of the entire letter. The interpreter of Paul's letters finds important clues by attending to the carefully composed paragraphs of thanksgiving.

(*c*) The body of the letter develops the themes. Because this part of the letter is so much longer than the comparable part of the ordinary Greek letter, there is reason to regard Paul's letters as "letter-essays" or "instructional letters." Since this part of the letter responds most directly to the issues among the readers, there is considerable diversity in the body of the various letters. Nonetheless, three features appear to be common to them all: (1) Subsections tend to build toward an eschatological note. (2) Paul includes his travel plans (Rom. 15:14–33; 1 Cor. 4:14–21; 1 Corinthians 16; 2 Cor. 12:14—13:13; Gal. 4:12–20; Phil. 2:19–24; Philemon 21–22). (3) Exhortations (i.e., *paraenesis*) usually appear near the end. The paraenesis includes a variety of topics not directly related to the argument. This is partly because Paul draws on traditions of moral counsel which touch a range of topics, and partly because Paul thinks certain admonitions are called for. The range of topics can be seen in Romans 12—13 or 1 Thess. 5:12–22.

(*d*) Paul also changes the letter-closing. In place of the wish for good health followed by "Farewell!" (*errōso*) Paul puts benedictions and doxologies. Both are rooted in the tradition of Jewish and emerging Christian worship—another indication of Paul's expectation that the letters would be read in worship. Several letters ask that readers greet one another with the "holy kiss" (Rom. 16:16; 1 Cor. 16:20; 2 Cor. 13:12; 1 Thess. 5:26). The concluding greetings to readers (sometimes named) were customary. Also customary is Paul's taking the stylus into his own hands to add a final note (1 Cor. 16:21–24; Gal. 6:11; Philemon 19). No trace of an original date remains; those given in some manuscripts are later guesses.

When Paul calls attention to what he himself writes, this is a sign that he probably dictated his letters. In only one instance do we know the scribe's name (Rom. 16:22—Tertius). We do not know whether Paul dictated word for word, or whether he told his scribe what to say but left the wording up to him. Paul sent the letter by personal courier, who probably also read it to the church and commented as he went along. There is a hint of this in Eph. 6:21–22 and Col. 4:7–8. When Paul's letters are read and interpreted in Christian worship, they are being used in their native habitat. Paul's letters are as at home in worship as a play is on stage.

Paul dictated his letters knowing that they would be read aloud to the house church. This explains why the letters contain so many rhetorical features. Scholars are resuming the analysis of the rhetorical character of Paul's letters. This work focuses on the body of the letter, where the arguments are developed. Long ago Rudolf Bultmann called attention to Paul's use of a particular rhetorical form, the *diatribē,* claiming that it had been developed by the Cynic-Stoic street preachers. Recently, however, Stowers has shown that its real home was not the street corner but the school. This conclusion accords better with the fact that Paul's letters were not designed to elicit conversion but to clarify and deepen the faith and ethics of those who had already responded. In the *diatribē* the speaker addressed an imaginary opponent, whose counterquestion set up the next point to be made by the speaker (somewhat like a "straight man" in a stand-up comedy). Romans 3:27–31 is a good example. At such passages, the interpreter should not conclude that Paul is answering actual objections raised by specific (though unnamed) opponents among the readers. Of course, Paul may have formulated the objections in light of his experience in debates.

Formal analysis of the Pauline letters is also concerned with the kind of argument Paul constructs overall. In antiquity, rhetoric was more a matter of argument than of ornament. Studying Paul's rhetoric, therefore, entails attending also to the strategy of his letters as a form of public discourse. In doing so, one assigns parts of the letters to the major parts of ancient discourses, such as *exordium* (opening remarks designed to establish rapport and set the direction of the speech), *narratio* (development of the argument) and its diverse components like summaries and digressions, and *peroratio*—each of which, according to ancient rhetorical theory, was to be developed in accord with the needs of a particular type of discourse. Hans Dieter Betz (*Galatians*) analyzes the text of Galatians in detail, assigning

to every sentence its role in the discourse according to major extant classical theorists of rhetoric. The very thoroughness of this analysis, however,
appears to put Paul's letter on a procrustean bed. Because Paul's letters
vary in length, mood, and purpose, other factors need to be considered as
well, including ancient instructions in letter writing (see Abraham J. Malherbe, *Ancient Epistolary Theorists*). As such work progresses, the nature
of Paul's letters as literary/rhetorical wholes will come into sharper focus.
In the long run, comparing Paul's letters with ancient rhetoric may be more
important for understanding his theology than comparing them with
ancient letters. Be that as it may, Paul created something new—a pastoral
letter to congregations.

The Foreground of the Letters

Just as there is a continuing debate over which aspect of Paul's cultural
background was most significant (see chap. 1), so there is an ongoing discussion over the nature of the problems with which Paul contended and
over the persons who generated them. Nor is it clear whether the difficulties in local congregations were expressions of a single phenomenon, or
whether Paul had to contend with quite different and unrelated problems.

For the interpreter the advantages of finding a single front are as clear
as the difficulties which result from finding multiple fronts; that is, the
more unified the issues the more coherent and unified Paul's theological
response. Conversely, the more diverse the issues, the greater the difficulty
of finding a common core. This is why the question before us has a direct
bearing on the way Paul's theology is portrayed.

Those who, following the lead of F. C. Baur (see above, p. 8), find the
key to Paul's theology in his tension with Jewish Christianity see the perva-
sive foreground in the trouble stirred up by Judaizers. The term
"Judaizers" does not appear in the NT itself but is formed from the verb
"Judaize" (Gal. 2:14; RSV: "live like a Jew"). Judaizers were Jewish
Christians who insisted that gentile believers must join the ethnic community of Israel in order to be bona fide Christians. How could one believe
that Jesus is the Messiah and not be part of the Messiah's people? Paul,
however, insisted that everyone becomes a member of the holy community
by faith; thereby he redefined that community. Judaizers regarded Paul,
therefore, as propagating a distorted gospel, and he returned the com-
pliment.

The conflict came to a head before Paul wrote the letters we have, and was to have been settled at "the Jerusalem Council" (Acts 15 and Galatians 2; see the recent discussion by Paul J. Achtemeier, *The Quest for Unity in the New Testament Church*). These differing accounts agree on the main point—male gentile Christians were not required to be circumcised—a rite by which one became a full-fledged Jew. Even though Paul's gospel was acknowledged by the council, problems continued because it had not been decided whether Jewish and gentile Christians could eat together. Some Jewish Christians arrived in Antioch and hectored the Jewish Christians so that they segregated themselves. Not even Peter and Barnabas, Paul's associates, could withstand the pressure. Paul reports all this to the Galatians because later the gentile Christians in Galatia were being persuaded to accept circumcision. Unfortunately for us, Paul did not identify who it was that was derailing the Galatians (he didn't have to since everybody then knew who it was). In Gal. 6:12-13 there is an intriguing characterization of them, but we still do not know who these people were or whether they had come from Jerusalem.

In Phil. 3:2-21 we see that Paul was contending with persons who took pride in their Jewishness and insisted on circumcision. In 2 Corinthians 10—13 we see that Paul's opposition in Corinth was Jewish (2 Cor. 11:22), though the word "circumcision" does not appear. Because in Romans Paul developed so fully his theology of justification by faith (apart from the law), one might infer that "Judaizers" got to Rome before Paul and had already discredited his gospel (see, e.g., Rom. 3:8, 31). In this way the conflict with "Judaizers" can be traced throughout the letters, and be made the single front against which Paul's theology was written.

Those who find the key to Paul's theology in his struggle with an early form of Gnosticism find some kind of gnostic under every bed. Such pan-Gnosticism has been advocated especially by Schmithals. He flatly denies that the instigators of the problem in Galatia were in any way dependent on Jerusalem Christianity (*Paul and the Gnostics,* 25); the challenge to Paul's apostleship does not come from that quarter but from gnostics who claim divine revelations. Those who were undermining Paul wherever he went were Jewish Christian gnostics from Asia Minor. The same gnostics who disdained Paul in Galatia and in Corinth were active also in Philippi. Since "no Judaizers emerged on the scene against Paul . . . Baur's construction of the history is dissolved" (ibid., 117).

Another way of positing continuity in the issues has been advocated often by Ernst Käsemann. His overarching term is "enthusiasm," a somewhat elusive concept. By "enthusiasm" Käsemann means more a stance than a particular group or theology. This stance emphasizes the radical newness of the Christian life, celebrates the "already" of salvation to the detriment of the "not yet," revels in the Spirit, and regards the sacraments as guarantees of salvation. Although Käsemann sees some sort of enthusiasm as endemic to Christianity from the start, what interests him is its development in Paul's Hellenistic churches, for which Corinth serves as the model. Paul himself cannot be isolated from it; indeed, he came into conflict with Palestinian Christians because "he has become the champion of the enthusiastic Hellenistic churches which were growing up free of the Law" (*Perspectives on Paul*, 125). Yet Paul was also intensely critical of enthusiasm when it became one-sided, and he relied on apocalyptic to counterweight it. In other words, Käsemann sees Paul as fighting against both enthusiasm and Judaistic legalism (*New Testament Questions of Today*, 254). By appealing to "enthusiasm" Käsemann penetrates to a deeper issue, the claim of all first-century Christians to be living in the power of the New Age; this claim in turn was expressed in various theologies and life styles. "Enthusiasm" allows Käsemann to incorporate the insight of the history of religion—that Hellenistic Christianity was deeply influenced by its environment through mystery cults, metaphysical dualism of body and spirit, and the myth of the divine redeemer—yet without simply making the Corinthians into gnostic Christians. Most important, by allowing Paul to share enthusiasm Käsemann anchors him firmly in Hellenistic Christianity; at the same time Käsemann regards Paul as its internal critic, always striving for a right balance between the "already" and the "not yet." Thus Paul becomes the great forerunner of the Reformation theme of *simul justus et peccator* (at the same time justified and a sinner).

Several conclusions can be drawn from this sketch:

(a) Inevitably the problems at Corinth have dominated the discussion. Not only does the sheer bulk of the Corinthian letters provide more evidence, but factoring out a number of earlier letters allows one to trace the history of Paul's problem in Corinth in a way that cannot be done elsewhere. Once a profile of the Corinthian church emerges, it is easy to find traces of the same problem elsewhere. However, it is far from clear that the issues remained the same even in Corinth. In 1 Corinthians the problems appear to be less severe than in 2 Corinthians 10—13, where it seems that outsiders have made matters worse. The actual situation was probably much more fluid and diverse than we can determine. If this was true of

Corinth, it is probably true also of Paul's other churches. It is interesting to note that most attempts to unify the front against which Paul fought often have trouble integrating 1 Thessalonians into the argument.

(*b*) Despite the danger of claiming to know too much, the value of such studies for the interpreter of Paul is clear. Negatively, they guard one against visualizing Paul as writing his theology out of his own musings, just as they prevent one from treating the occasion of the letters as a mere catalyst which triggered Paul's thinking. Positively, these efforts allow us to see Paul at work, struggling with alternate interpretations of the gospel being advocated by real people. Paul himself emerges as an intensely human apostle, and his theology as a dynamic process constantly interacting with the stance of Christians just as committed as he was.

The Background of the Letters

Just as Paul's foreground determined what he had to discuss, so his background affected how he would say it and the resources at his disposal. The theology of the letters articulates the specific interaction of these elements; the rest of Paul's theology remains largely hidden from us, apart from allusions. Here we will concentrate on his personal background and his use of traditions.

Although some scholars have doubted that Paul had been a student of Gamaliel in Jerusalem (Acts 22:3), it is impossible to doubt the statement in Acts 26:5—that Paul had been a Pharisee—because Paul himself confirms it (Phil. 3:5; Gal. 1:14). Precisely what "Pharisee" meant in Paul's case is not self-evident because of two considerations: One, he was a diaspora Jew who according to Acts (16:37; 22:28) was a Roman citizen from birth; his letters always use his Roman name, Paulus. Two, Pharisaism in Paul's early years differed from the rabbinism which developed after the fall of Jerusalem in A.D. 70. Hence one must be cautious in using second-century rabbinic texts to describe pre-70 Pharisaism. Nonetheless, it is certain that he had been a Pharisee, zealous for the Torah.

Equally important, Paul remembers that he had tried to destroy Christianity. Curiously, he never reveals what prompted him to undertake that project (1 Cor. 15:9; Gal. 1:13). Since Judaism seems to have tolerated a rather broad spectrum of beliefs, including views of who the Messiah would be, it is unlikely that what set Paul into motion was only the belief that the Messiah was Jesus. It is more likely that Paul saw the developing freedom with regard to the law, especially among the Hellenistic Jewish

Christians, as a threat to Judaism and as an affront to God. Then he turned around: the persecutor became propagator. Paul never describes his "conversion," though he refers to it as a revelation of God's Son (Gal. 1:16); nor does he tell us where or when it occurred. All discussion of his Damascus road experience depends on Acts (9:1–19; 22:4–16; 26:9–18). (See Beverly Roberts Gaventa, *From Darkness to Light: Aspects of Conversion in the New Testament.*)

Paul did not separate the experience of coming to faith from knowing himself to be called by God to be an apostle to the Gentiles. His conversion and his call coincided (Gal. 1:15–16). Because Paul did not have this experience as the result of an extended religious quest, nor under the tutelage of a mentor or guru, he regarded his coming to faith as an act of God, as divine intervention to rescue a persecutor from self-destruction. It was an act of God's grace. This meant that Paul also regarded his gospel as divinely authorized, as the Word of God (1 Thess. 2:13). To challenge Paul's gospel was to challenge his authorization, his warrant; to challenge his warrant was to challenge his gospel. So intimate was the connection between the man and the message that Paul insisted that his apostolic status was dependent on God only (Gal. 1:1, 12); he was Christ's own apostle, not a legate or emissary of the church. He believed God himself was calling his hearers to faith through his word (2 Cor. 5:20). It is essential to see that for Paul it is not he who legitimates his gospel (it is true because it is Paul's), but it is the gospel that legitimates Paul (Paul is an apostle because the gospel is true).

Sometimes Paul's theology has been regarded as simply an explication of his experience. This is as difficult to deny as it is to demonstrate, the former because it is hard to sunder the man from the message, the latter because Paul never grounds his theological arguments in his conversion experience. Rarely does he refer to his religious experiences of any kind (1 Cor. 9:1; 2 Cor. 12:1–10; Gal. 1:12–17; 2:2), and all of these are in polemical discussions in which he defends his authorization. Nor does Paul say that his theology was revealed to him (1 Thess. 4:15 might imply this, but might also refer to a tradition). Though he can speak in tongues, he does not regard his letters as "translations" of what he heard or uttered in ecstasy. Nonetheless, a Pharisee whose zeal led him to persecute a new faith among fellow Jews, and who then turned about and advocated what he had tried to destroy, and who regarded this transformation as God's

act—such a person can scarcely develop any other kind of theology than
one which emphasized the radicality of God's grace and power.

Difficult as it is to discern precisely how Paul's conversion experience
is linked to this theological thinking, it is even more difficult to see how
his apostolic experience affected his thought. The time span between Paul's
conversion (around A.D. 35) and the earliest letter we have (around A.D.
50/51) is greater than the period during which the letters we know were
written (ca. A.D. 51–57, assuming that no parts of our Philippians were
written from Rome). This earlier period is totally hidden from us, yet it
probably consisted of the same sort of activities we see later: traveling in
dangerous circumstances, teaching in synagogues where he was more often
repudiated than not and where he was three times officially punished with
thirty-nine lashes, baptizing those who accepted his message, nurturing the
new community in house churches by explaining the meaning of it all in
light of the synagogue Bible—all the while working for a living (see 2 Cor.
11:23–29; 1 Thess. 2:1–12). The man who wrote the seven letters was no
novice, but a seasoned teacher-pastor who had had ample occasion to
develop a repertoire of phrases, arguments, and ways of appealing to Scripture. Even though Paul's letters respond to concrete situations, we need not
think that every line is a fresh creation. It is likely that Paul reformulated
and rethought things he had said before, perhaps often. This may account,
in part, for the compact style in certain passages.

In short, the personal background of each letter is the entire career of
Paul up to the moment of dictation. If the whole of Paul's thought is never
visible, even in the aggregate, Paul himself is nonetheless authentically
present, revealing a good deal about himself while rarely making himself
the subject matter of the letters.

The other factor in the background of the letters consists of the traditions
Paul used. Paul relied on older material more often than he indicated—1
Cor. 11:23–25 (the Lord's Supper) and 15:3–7 (resurrection appearances).
In both cases he used fixed formulations and therefore introduced them
with the Greek equivalent of technical rabbinic terms for receiving
(*paralambanō*) and delivering (*paradidōmi*) tradition. It is likely that he
received these traditions when he became a member of the church, just as
it is likely that the traditions themselves had been formulated by the
Hellenistic Jewish Christians in Damascus or Antioch, who in turn relied,
in part, on motifs and phrases used in Palestine.

Careful attention to vocabulary and rhythmic phrasing has led to the conclusion that Paul quoted material also at other points. There is broad consensus that Phil. 2:6–11 is a Christ-hymn, and that Rom. 1:3–5 contains a confession (or part of one). The same holds true of Rom. 3:25, though Rom. 4:25 may be Paul's own rhetorically balanced formulation. Romans 10:9 also looks like a traditional formulation, as does Gal. 3:20–21. First Corinthians 13 is often regarded as an "ode to love" which Paul found appropriate to use here. First Corinthians 15:33, 2 Cor. 9:6, and Gal. 5:9 are proverbs, and 1 Cor. 15:32 is a popular slogan that looks like a parody of the Epicurean attitude toward death. First Corinthians 3:17a has been called a "sentence of holy law," identified by Käsemann as a retribution formula used by early Christian prophets (*New Testament Questions of Today*, 66–81). Romans 1:29–31 is a list of vices probably taken from Hellenized Judaism; comparable lists are found in popular moral literature of the time. The same is true of 1 Cor. 6:9–10. First Thessalonians 4:13–5:11 is an extended piece of apocalyptic instruction. Paul's ethical injunctions probably use pieces of tradition characterized by terse imperatives (Rom. 12:9–21; 2 Cor. 13:11; 1 Thess. 5:14–22). There are also instances where Paul used inherited exegetical materials; one example is the *catena* (chain) of OT quotations in Rom. 3:10–18. (Paul's use of the words of Jesus will concern us in chap. 3.)

In the recent years, there has been a clear upsurge in efforts to identify not only post-Pauline additions to the texts but also Paul's own dependence on earlier materials. Indeed, in a few cases such as Rom. 3:24–26 or 1 Thess. 2:14–16, what one person regards as pre-Pauline tradition another calls an interpolation. This is partly because in both cases the evidence—differing vocabulary and point of view—for the one can be adduced also on behalf of the other hypothesis. What tips the scale in favor of Paul's own use of earlier material is the extent to which it is integral to the argument. The more integrated, the stronger the likelihood that Paul himself included it. The same consideration, however, makes it difficult to distinguish when Paul's own language draws on earlier material (as in a paraphrase) from when he simply incorporates sentences congenial with his own thought. It would be easier to factor the Pauline letters into three strata—pre-Pauline, Pauline, and post-Pauline—if we had a more precise use of the word "tradition," and if it were used consistently. In what follows, "tradition" will be reserved for *traditum*—what has been handed down in a stable formulation; "traditional" will be used for passages where one suspects that Paul is not creating fresh sentences but drawing on inherited (and perhaps common) phrases or motifs.

For example, in 1 Cor. 15:27-28 Paul interprets Ps. 110:1, widely used by early Christians to interpret Jesus' exaltation in resurrection. The inferences drawn from this psalm are Paul's own, but associating the psalm with Jesus' resurrection was "traditional," customary. Likewise in 1 Cor. 10:4 Paul Christianizes a rabbinic interpretation of two stories in the OT (Exod. 17:1-17; Num. 20:1-13). Jewish exegetes had inferred that although both stories refer to a wondrous rock, there was only one rock, and therefore the rock followed the Israelites. Paul assumes all this, and simply identifies the rock as Christ. In cases like this, the tacit understandings are traditional, but what appears in Paul's letters are not pieces of fixed tradition, but his own free use of inherited motifs.

Discovering the extent to which Paul adopted and adapted pieces of tradition, traditional modes of thought, and motifs helps the interpreter overcome the notion—ultimately grounded in Romanticism—that Paul was a solitary, original genius who created his theological understanding out of his own depths. Paul's "depths" were indeed plumbed as he wrote, but his creativity consisted largely in his capacity to give traditions and traditional material new significance by expounding their implications for the situations he confronted. Paul was a bearer and refractor of multiple traditions and inherited motifs.

Considerable effort has been devoted to recovering the wording of the traditions in order to analyze them in their own right so that Paul can be located more precisely on the map of early Christianity. Although the data are limited, Paul emerges as the interpreter of traditions formed in that strand of Christianity which developed among Hellenized Jews and Gentiles, probably centered in Antioch. In the deutero-Pauline letters we see how Paul himself became traditional material for the next generation.

Paul's clear reliance on earlier materials is one important side of the theme "Paul and tradition." The other side concerns his freedom. This manifests itself not only in the wide range of resources upon which he drew, Christian and non-Christian, but also in his freedom to modify and reinterpret what he used. It is widely believed, for instance, that he added "even death on a cross" to the hymn in Phil. 2:8 (and perhaps other phrases as well). In 1 Cor. 11:26 he comments on the Lord's Supper tradition, and in 1 Cor. 15:8 he does not hesitate to add his own name to the roster of those to whom Christ appeared. He also seems to have expanded the confessional formula in Rom. 1:3–5 and 3:24–26. For Paul, this older material was not a holy object to be handed on with reverence like a talisman. Nor is Paul bound by earlier formulations as if they had been revealed. Rather, he moves among these multiple traditions with sovereign freedom. The letters show what happened when these materials passed through the mind of Paul.

PART II

THE GOSPEL PAUL PREACHED

How Paul preached the gospel when he arrived in a town remains largely unknown. The Book of Acts gives two sample sermons, one of his preaching in Hellenistic synagogues (Acts 13:13–41), the other of his preaching to gentile intellectuals (Acts 17:22–31). Since both fit so neatly the perspective of Acts, only with great caution can one use them to portray Paul's own preaching. That must be inferred from his letters.

The letters do not summarize what Paul preached to elicit faith, but interpret aspects of that preaching and its foundations. In developing his arguments, he alludes to this prior preaching/teaching; these references furnish the foundation of any reconstruction of Paul's preaching. To them we can add the traditions and traditional materials, motifs, and arguments that we noted in chapter 2 because readers would have recognized some of this material as part of Paul's earlier teaching.

We shall discuss three themes: the pivotal event of Jesus Christ (chap. 3); the salvific response Paul elicited (chap. 4); and the theological horizons of his proclamation (chap. 5). A sharp distinction between the gospel Paul preached and the theological issues he developed and defended in the letters cannot be maintained, of course. Nonetheless, two things should emerge from these chapters: (1) a sketch of Paul's message, and (2) an outline of the substratum on which the epistles rest.

CHAPTER THREE

THE PIVOTAL EVENT

Paul called his message "gospel" (*euangelion*). Our word "evangelist" comes from the same word-family, yet Paul never calls himself an evangelist. His customary self-designation is "apostle" (*apostolos*), a sent-one—an emissary sent by God to preach the gospel. It was the gospel that lay at the core of his self-understanding and of his life work (1 Thess. 2:4). Everything else was subservient to it.

Apparently it was Paul who introduced the term *euangelion* into the Christian vocabulary. Etymologically, *euangelion* is good news. *Euangelion* was not a common religious term in antiquity, neither among Greeks nor Jews. Interestingly, an inscription uses it in connection with the cult of the emperor: "The birthday of the god [the emperor] was for the world the beginning of good announcements" (plural of *euangelion*). It is disputed whether this meaning influenced early Christian usage; in any case, for Christians there is only one *euangelion*. The plural is never used of the proclamation. The LXX, the Greek translation of the Bible made in Alexandria several centuries before Paul, uses the verb for announcements of God's eschatological deed, the coming of salvation (e.g., as quoted in Rom. 10:15). How the noun *euangelion* came into Paul's vocabulary remains obscure, but the fact that he could write simply of "the gospel" shows that he assumed his readers knew what he was talking about (e.g., Rom. 10:16; 1 Cor. 15:1). Paul uses *euangelion* more than any other NT writer.

Paul sometimes characterizes this gospel. When he calls it "the gospel of God" (Rom. 1:1; 2 Cor. 11:7; 1 Thess. 2:2, 8, 9), he means both the gospel that comes from God and the gospel about God, for the two cannot be separated neatly. When he calls it "the gospel of Christ" (e.g., Rom. 15:19; 1 Cor. 9:12; 2 Cor. 2:12; 10:14; 1 Thess. 3:2), however, he does not refer to Christ's own message but to the message whose content is Christ. When Paul writes of "my [or 'our'] gospel" (Rom. 2:16; 16:25; 2 Cor. 4:3; 1 Thess. 1:5) he does not imply that he has a message peculiar to himself;

he simply means the gospel he preached (as Gal. 1:11; 2:2 show). Precisely in Galatians, where Paul must defend his gospel, he never calls it "my gospel," but insists that there is only one gospel (Gal. 1:6–8). Evidently Paul allowed for some latitude in theological formulation so long as the heart of the matter—what he calls "the truth of the gospel" (Gal. 2:5, 14 [5:7]) was not jeopardized, for there was only a single gospel. What his opponents later propagated in Galatia and Corinth was really "another gospel" (Gal. 1:7; 2 Cor. 11:4)—a self-contradiction sufficient to disqualify it.

Paul regarded his message as something radical and decisive, not as religious suggestions for better living, or as one more possibility alongside the many cults and religions of the day. Nor did Paul see himself propagating a new religion; whether in fact he was doing so is a modern historian's judgment. For Paul the gospel message was God's power that effected salvation (Rom. 1:16). Although it is an announcement of an event, it is not merely information about it. Although it is a word from and about God, and so is eminently theological, it is not merely theology either. Rather, the message itself has power wherever it is believed. Moreover, it was accompanied by events of power, what we might call "miracles" (2 Cor. 12:12; 1 Thess. 1:5), and by the powerful manifestations of God's Spirit among those who accepted the gospel and were baptized. Paul regarded these accompaniments as confirmation of the power of the message to transform human life. The gospel announced what God had done through the event we call "Jesus Christ." The remainder of this chapter will explore three aspects of Paul's gospel-presentation of the Christ-event: the cross/resurrection; the relation of Paul to Jesus and to the early tradition of Jesus' teachings; and finally Paul's understanding of the pre-existence of Christ.

Cross and Resurrection

The message that Paul preached to gentile hearers included an appeal to abandon the worship of the gods and "to serve a living and true God" (1 Thess. 1:9). This motif was shared with the Jewish synagogue, as was the appeal to the OT as God's revelation. What distinguished Paul's message from that of the synagogue, and from that of other traveling preachers, was the way he presented the event of Jesus. This is clear in how Paul continues—"and to wait for his Son from heaven, whom he raised from the dead, Jesus who delivers us from the wrath to come." This passage is not a compendium of the themes of Paul's preaching; it highlights the future aspects of it in keeping with the problem to be addressed later, the Christian hope. Jesus is identified as God's Son who, having been raised from the dead and exalted to heavenly status, will come as deliverer from the great judgment ("the wrath to come"). In other words, the focus is on the salvific meaning of the Jesus-event, which is more than the lifetime of Jesus. In 1 Cor. 2:2, where Paul identified the focus of his preaching to the Corinthians, he wrote, "I decided to know nothing among you except Jesus Christ and him crucified"—clearly indicating the core was Christ and that Christ was presented from the angle of the crucifixion. The fact that 1 Thess. 1:10 (and Rom. 10:9) mentions only Jesus' resurrection, and 1 Cor. 2:2 only the cross, does not mean that Paul shifted content. Rather, because cross and resurrection constituted a single meaning-complex, Paul could mention one and imply the other, depending on which aspect was most germane to the point being made at the moment.

One of the most important texts in the NT is 1 Cor. 15:3-11, where Paul quotes a fixed tradition (see chap. 2): "Christ died for our sins in accordance with the scriptures, he was buried, he was raised on the third day in accordance with the scriptures." This tradition was made the foundation of Paul's preaching in Corinth and elsewhere. Several things strike us about the way this old tradition speaks of the Jesus-event: (a) Since Christ means Messiah, the formulation expresses a drastic transformation of Jewish expectation. Attempts to find Jewish precedents for the idea that the Messiah would die to atone for sin have failed. (b) Christ's death is not understood as a tragedy that befell a good man, a miscarriage of justice, nor as a model of self-giving. Rather it is an event through which sin is effectively dealt with. (c) To say that both Christ's death and God's act of resurrecting him (the passive "was raised" implies that God did the resurrecting; Jesus did not "rise" from the dead) are in accord with Scripture is to call for a reexamination of Scripture, for a particular way of interpreting it. (d) Nothing is said about Christ's identity as God's Son, nor of the virgin birth, ministry, and teaching of Jesus. The focus is not on information about Jesus but on the salvific meaning of the event, focused on its outcome—death and resurrection.

That the core of Paul's preaching was Jesus' cross and resurrection as God's way of dealing with sin is clearly implied also by the way Paul writes to the Roman church which had not yet heard him preach. In this epistle Paul appropriates materials from Hellenistic Jewish Christianity, and assumes that the readers will recognize that his exposition of the gospel accords with those materials. Romans 3:24–26 contains such traditional language. We need not decide precisely which phrases Paul inherited and which he contributed to the passage. Paul wrote of "the redemption which is in Christ Jesus, whom God has put forward as an expiation by his blood" (i.e., death). The word *hilastērion* (RSV: "expiation") can also be translated "mercy seat," an allusion to the lid of the sacred box, the ark of the covenant, in the Jerusalem temple. On the Day of Atonement this lid was sprinkled with sacrificial blood as part of the ritual by which God's forgiveness was granted and claimed. It is disputed whether Paul (or the tradition) meant "whom God put forward as a mercy seat by his blood"; probably "expiation" is correct. An expiation is not a propitiation. The latter is something that ameliorates wrath, dissolves hostility by placating the aggrieved; the former expunges, takes away sin. The point is that Christ's death does not do something that turns God's wrath away but something that deals with sin. The problem is not the disposition of God but the condition of humanity. This tightly compressed paragraph uses language taken from the Jewish sacrificial system to interpret Jesus' death as a sacrifice that deals with sin. How that occurs is not explained. In appropriating this tradition, Paul shows that he too understands Christ's death as atonement. The same is true of Rom. 4:24–25, which speaks of the resurrection of Jesus "who was put to death for our transgressions and raised for our justification." Here the RSV's "was put to death" translates *paredothē*, "was handed over" (by God). The same verb is used in the Lord's Supper tradition (1 Cor. 11:23), where the customary translation is "betrayed"; it could also be translated as "on the night when he was handed over" (by God, not by Judas).

What has emerged so far? Although the message Paul presented in order to elicit faith included a variety of themes such as monotheism, Scripture, and the coming judgment, the core was the particular interpretation of the Jesus-event, and its focal point was the cross and resurrection. Just as Paul can oscillate between mentioning the cross and the resurrection without splitting them apart, so he can shift from saying that Christ gave himself (Gal. 1:4, 20) to saying that God gave him over to death (Rom. 4:25). Christ's act was God's act: "God shows his love for us in that while we were yet sinners Christ died for us" (Rom. 5:8). This paradoxical way of speaking should not be glossed over, for together with the tradition in 1 Cor. 15:3, it expressed an understanding of God and Jesus which is constitutive for Paul's gospel (and for the type of Christianity in which it is rooted).

We do not know how the earliest Christians reasoned toward the formulations we now have in Paul's letters. Probably their starting point was not the incarnation but the resurrection. How might they have arrived at the convictions which are distilled in these formulations?

They did not begin in a vacuum, of course. As Jews, they already believed that sacrificial death and forgiveness of sins go together—an age-old connection. Given this assumption, they might have reasoned as follows: (*a*) God's resurrecting Jesus vindicates Jesus. (*b*) Those who believe that God has done this know themselves to be rightly related to God, forgiven; those who refuse to believe this are still at odds with God, though they think otherwise. (*c*) It is God's purpose that sin be dealt with and that persons be rightly related to God. (*d*) Since the new right relation to God results from the resurrection, and since the resurrection would not have occurred apart from Jesus' death, Jesus' execution must be God's means of bringing about the new relationship. (*e*) Because to be granted a new relationship to God is to become the beneficiary of God's love, Christ's death must also be an act of God's love, since precisely this new relationship to God would not have occurred apart from the cross/resurrection. (*f*) Consequently one can say that "Christ died for our sins." Whether or not these were the steps by which Christians came to the conclusions behind the tradition in 1 Corinthians 15 and Paul's statement in Rom. 5:8, these formulations are outcroppings of a rather sophisticated understanding of Jesus' death. The gospel is not theology, but it implies a particular theological understanding of God, Christ, and the human situation. (See also Arland J. Hultgren, *Christ and His Benefits*, 47–57.)

Paul's gospel was not presented simply as the answer to the religious quests of his hearers, but as the God-given announcement of an event whose meaning challenges those quests, at least the terms in which they were pursued. Paul characterized his gospel of the cross as "folly to those who are perishing"; it is a "stumbling block to Jews and folly to Gentiles" (1 Cor. 1:18, 22). The gospel challenged the prevailing understandings of God, the human condition, and the means of dealing with it. The gospel called for a reconstruction of those understandings.

Paul and the Traditions of the Pivotal Event

For Paul, the gospel is a heraldic announcement of an event, of a piece of history (the cross) inseparably linked with something that, strictly speaking, is not history at all—the resurrection. At the same time, in Paul's day there were circulating traditions about both Jesus' ministry and about the resurrection appearances. How was the gospel Paul preached related to these traditions?

Paul apparently never saw or heard Jesus (1 Cor. 9:1 refers to a vision of the resurrected Lord), and no one "saw" the resurrection. What Paul knew about Jesus depended either on reports and formulated traditions or on his immediate experience of the Lord. There were no written gospels in Paul's day. The collection of Jesus' sayings (Q) used by both Matthew and Luke was circulating then, probably in Palestine-Syria, but there is no reason to think that Paul used it. The question of Paul's relation to the Jesus-traditions has been debated intensely in Pauline study. We shall note the major positions taken after we have looked at Paul himself.

1. What did Paul know about Jesus' crucifixion and resurrection? (a) Paul says almost nothing about the crucifixion except that it occurred. None of the details that appear in any of our Gospel accounts are mentioned by Paul—assuming that *paredothē* in 1 Cor. 11:23 means "handed over by God," not "betrayed" (i.e., by Judas). Since 1 Thess. 2:14–16 is an interpolation we cannot say that Paul blamed either the Jews or the Romans for the crucifixion. According to 1 Cor. 2:8, those who "crucified the Lord of glory" were "the rulers of this age"—apparently meaning that the invisible malign principalities and powers were at work in this event, using earthly agents. Paul has no interest in the earthly agents themselves (*we* connect them with Pilate and Caiaphas because we have the Gospels). When Paul mentions "Christ, our paschal lamb" (1 Cor. 5:7), he probably reflects knowledge that Christ's death occurred during Passover, but he gives no other information about the event itself. (b) Paul's knowledge of the resurrection is somewhat different. In 1 Cor. 15:8 he included himself in the tradition about those to whom the Lord was made visible; that makes him "an eyewitness" of the appearances, on a par with the others. But Paul never describes the Lord he saw. Nor does he ever mention the empty tomb. Nor does the list of appearances in the tradition quoted in 1 Corinthians 15 coincide with the appearance stories in the Gospels; the closest agreement is the trace of the fact that the Lord first appeared to Peter (Luke 24:34; Mark 16:7). It is sometimes said that because the tradition mentioned the burial (1 Cor. 15:4) Paul must have known that the tomb was empty because Jews could scarcely have believed otherwise if a buried man was resurrected. Yet the fact remains that Paul never mentions the tomb at

all. We who have the Gospels have more resurrection traditions than Paul mentions, and some of those he mentions are not found in the Gospels (the appearance to the five hundred and to James, Jesus' brother).

2. What did Paul know about Jesus prior to his execution? This is exceedingly difficult to determine, because all we know is what Paul mentions. Paul knew, of course, that Jesus was a Jew. According to Rom. 9:5, he was an Israelite, a descendant of Abraham according to Gal. 3:16, and a son of David according to Rom. 1:3. He was born "under the law" (Gal. 4:4). Each of these references, however, is in the service of a theological point, and does not simply state a "historical fact." Paul also knew that Jesus had brothers (1 Cor. 9:5), one of whom was James, the head of the Jerusalem church (Gal. 1:19). That did not give James special standing in Paul's eyes, though he recognizes that this made James a "pillar" in the eyes of others (Gal. 2:6, 9). Paul also knew that Jesus' mission was among his own people (Rom. 15:8), something that could be assumed. Paul never mentions the virgin birth, Jesus' baptism by John (though Acts 13:24–25 has him do so), nor any of the deeds of Jesus' ministry.

3. What did Paul know about Jesus' teaching? If we had only Paul's letters, we would never know that Jesus told parables, nor that he had preached the news of the kingdom. What strikes many students as especially problematic is that even when Paul writes about things that Jesus also discussed (e.g., food laws or taxes to Rome), Paul does not mention Jesus' teaching (Mark 7:1–23, which includes later material; 12:13–17). Even if Paul knew the Lord's Prayer (Rom. 8:15), he does not associate it with Jesus. What Paul does cite as Jesus' word is a saying about divorce (1 Cor. 7:10–11), support for preachers of the gospel (1 Cor. 9:14) and the coming of the Lord (1 Thess. 4:15–17). It is not clear whether "the word of the Lord" in 1 Thess. 4:15–17 is a tradition (or rests on traditional materials) from the pre-Easter Jesus or a word of the risen Lord. In 1 Cor. 9:14 we have not a quotation but a statement of the point: "Those who proclaim the gospel should get their living by the gospel," something that accords with Matt. 10:10 and Luke 10:7–8 but is not verbally identical with either one. In 1 Cor. 7:10–11, he knows the Markan form of Jesus' teaching which forbids both husband and the wife to divorce (Mark 10:10–12; compare Matt. 5:31–32; 19:9; Luke 16:18). Paul also distinguishes sharply what the Lord says ("Not I but the Lord," v. 10) from what Paul himself says ("I say, not the Lord," v. 12), an indication that the tradition of the Lord's teaching is being taken very seriously.

This remarkable (to us!) absence of Jesus' teaching from Paul's letters, and of the total neglect of his ministry and the limited reference to his passion have spawned various explanations which tend to be one of two types. The first regards the evidence of the letters as misleading and argues that Paul knew, and valued what he knew, more about Jesus than the letters show. The second regards the evidence of the letters as a quite accurate reflection of Paul's attitude. We will look briefly at both.

The attempt to show that the Jesus-traditions were actually more important to Paul than the number of references in the letters indicates is usually built on three considerations. One emphasizes the occasional character of the letters; that is, since the letters are written to those who had already heard Paul preach, and since the letters discuss specific issues in the churches, the few references to the pre-Easter Jesus are not an index of his importance for Paul's own theology and preaching. Another appeals to Paul's two-week visit with Peter in Jerusalem (Gal. 1:18)—ample time to acquire a body of information about Jesus. This argument has not won widespread support. The third contends that there are numerous allusions to Jesus' teachings in Paul's letters—not quotations or paraphrases, but signs of influence. For instance, David Stanley (*Catholic Biblical Quarterly* 23 [1961]) argued that Rom. 13:7 alludes to Matt. 22:21; Rom. 13:8–10 alludes to Jesus' teaching about the great commandment (Mark 12:28–34), Rom. 8:15 to the Lord's Prayer; Rom. 14:14 rests on Matt. 15:11, 20; and Rom. 4:4–5 alludes to the parable of the laborers in the vineyard (Matt. 20:1–16). Recently, Dale Allison, Jr., argued that Paul actually knew collections of Jesus' sayings (*New Testament Studies* 28 [1982], 1–32).

The more one studies such attempts to locate allusions, the more skeptical one becomes. The first consideration is the most significant. That is, there is no reason to think that Paul mentioned everything he knew about Jesus in letters addressed to specific occasions. Still, it is one thing to affirm, whether as a hunch or as a conviction, that Paul knew more about Jesus than he says, and another to be able to show it.

On the other hand, it has been argued that in principle Paul was not interested in "the historical Jesus," so that even if he had known more information he would not have used it. This view, advocated already by Albert Schweitzer, was developed especially by Rudolf Bultmann. Since it has been rather influential, it is useful to examine it more closely. (*a*) Bultmann rightly saw that Paul's theology is neither an extension nor an elaboration of Jesus' own message. Paul did not see himself as Jesus' successor.

Moreover, a report of Jesus' words and deeds did not constitute the core of Paul's gospel. (b) Paul did not regard Jesus as an example to be followed; indeed, the motif of discipleship is virtually absent from Paul. (c) There is, however, fundamental congruity between Jesus and Paul with regard to the human situation before God. Their vocabulary was different, but what each was expressing existentially was the same. "Jesus says nothing other in his call to repentance than Paul tries to make clear in his theology by means of theoretical argument" ("Jesus and Paul," in *Existence and Faith,* 188). (d) Yet, there is a difference: Jesus looked forward to the coming of the kingdom but Paul looked back to what had already occurred as the decisive event (cross/resurrection). Still, Bultmann did not account historically for this existential congruity between Jesus and Paul. (e) Later, Bultmann appealed to 2 Cor. 5:16-17 to argue that Paul was not interested in a "fleshly Christ," that is, the historical Jesus. But it is almost certain that when Paul wrote of knowing Christ "according to the flesh" the phrase "according to the flesh" modifies the verb, not the noun—Paul writes about a way of knowing, not about the known.

Bultmann's view expresses a theological position—genuine faith exists only vis-à-vis the word of God, a reality that cannot be investigated as if it were a phenomenon. A "Christ according to the flesh," a "historical Jesus," however, he regarded as precisely such an investigatable phenomenon. Hence Paul, anticipating Bultmann, saw that it would be theologically illegitimate to have included a report of the words and deeds of Jesus in his preaching of the gospel. On the whole, Bultmann is more correct in what he denies—the liberal Protestant concern to make a heroic account of Jesus' words and deeds the core of the gospel—than in what he affirms: Paul in principle is not interested in the Jesus of history.

Summary

My views can be summarized as follows:

1. It is futile to try to expand the range of the Jesus-traditions known to Paul by looking for allusions. We must try to understand Paul's relation to the Jesus-tradition on another basis.

2. For Paul the words of Jesus were important as church regulations, not as gospel proclamation, kerygma. Even when Paul cites the Jesus-tradition, he does not introduce it as the words of Jesus but as the words of the Lord; that is, through the tradition the living Lord continues to address the church. Paul did not draw as sharp a line, as we often do,

between what Jesus once said and what he now says (which is not to say that he obliterated the difference altogether).

3. This means that for Paul what matters is the event as a whole, not individual segments of it, whether incidents or sayings. What is important for Paul is what God did through the event (cross/resurrection), not what Jesus *NB* himself had said or done in God's name. To have anchored his theology there would have shifted the whole discussion to another theme—Jesus' own authority. For Paul, however, the cross is not simply an incident, nor an isolable occurrence, but the capstone and epitome of the event as a whole. How Paul understood that event now needs to be brought into view.

The Shape of the Pivotal Event

Paul's understanding of the Christ-event is grasped only when it is perceived in its entirety—that is, when what we call "the historical Jesus" is seen as part of an event that transcends the beginning as well as the end of his life. In other words, the "historical Jesus" is framed by the pre-existence of God's Son and the post-existence of the resurrected one.

Pre-existence

It may be useful here to reflect on the term "pre-existence" because it is difficult for us to conceive of something being before it exists. Many ancients did not have this difficulty. They believed, just as we do, that "existence" characterized the world of time-space. For them this phenomenal, empirical existence of time-space was not the only reality, however. There was another reality, another "dimension," so to speak. Whereas existence in time-space was real, the other existence was "really real," eternal rather than temporal. In Jewish thought, certain things existed in this super-real existence before they became temporal events (e.g., the name of the Messiah or the Torah). The function of this kind of thinking was to be able to say that important realities in human experience have a transcendent origin, and are not simply the outcome of historical, mundane factors interacting with one another. Thus the Torah was indeed given through Moses, but the Torah itself is not a historical reality but is as eternal and as transcendent as the mind and will of God. It "was" before it "became." The Jewish theologian, Philo, found Platonic thinking about eternal ideas, of which earthly actualities are copies, congenial to interpret the eternal nature of the Torah. In short, whereas we may need to struggle to think in such terms, many theologians in antiquity took the category "pre-existence" for granted. Paul certainly did, and his letters never justify using it. (For a contrary view, see James D. G. Dunn, *Christology in the Making.*)

The more one believed that God radically transcended the world of time-space, the more important became a mediator, an agent, through whom God created and ordered the world. In Hellenized Judaism, this mediatorial role was played by Sophia, Wisdom. Because Wisdom was understood to be virtually interchangeable with God's will and word, it was easy to infer that God created the world through Wisdom. Two centuries before Paul, the Wisdom of Solomon could celebrate Sophia as the radiation of God himself. She (Sophia is a feminine noun) enters human souls each generation "and makes them friends of God, and prophets" (Wisd. of Sol. 7:27). The word "radiation" (both the process and what is radiated) used of Sophia was later used of the pre-existent Christ by the author of Hebrews; the RSV renders the word as "he reflects the glory of God." In short, what Heb. 1:1–3a says about the pre-existent Son of God, Hellenized Jewish theology had said previously about Sophia and her relation to the world. The same background shaped Col. 1:15–16.

When NT authors wrote of the pre-existence of Christ, they were applying to him a sophisticated way of thinking which was deeply established in Hellenized Judaism, which in turn was deeply influenced by Greek thought. Paul could assume that he need not explain or justify speaking of an eternal reality which manifested itself in time-space. Because it "was" before it "became," it could be spoken of as *pre*-existing. What early Christians claimed was that this pre-existing reality became Jesus. They did not hold that Jesus pre-existed; rather what pre-existed was God's Son who became Jesus. All incarnational Christology rests on such a conceptual basis.

Apparently Hellenistic Jewish Christianity first developed incarnational Christology. Instead of saying that Jesus was installed into his messianic office at resurrection (as Acts 2:36 states), or that he was anointed Son of God at his baptism (as Mark 1:9–11 reports), or that Jesus was Son of God from the moment of conception onward, as the Matthean and Lukan stories suggest, incarnational Christology begins prior to the existence of Jesus and regards his life as a phase in the role of the Son of God. The fact that already Paul assumes such a three-step Christology (pre-existence, existence, post-existence) shows that these modes of thinking about Christ existed side by side almost from the start. It would be another century before these modes would be combined into the orthodox Christology, according to which the incarnation of the pre-existent Son of God occurred at the wondrous conception in Mary's womb. In the NT itself, no one put all of the elements together this way.

Before looking more closely at Paul's understanding of the Christ-event, several general observations are appropriate. (*a*) There are no passages in the letters designed to instruct the readers in Christology. Christological statements, even the longer ones, always appear where something else is discussed. Although christological issues were deeply involved in Paul's controversies, Christology proper (e.g., appropriate titles for Jesus, incarnation) does not seem to have been the issue. (*b*) This means that Paul's christological statements do not constitute a peculiarly Pauline Christology. Rather, they express a characteristically Pauline interpretation of christological motifs, categories, and titles which were widely shared in Hellenistic gentile and Hellenistic Jewish Christianity. (*c*) Consequently, Paul's Christology was part of the gospel he proclaimed and taught. Without a Christology he could scarcely have proclaimed his gospel at all. Therefore we discuss Paul's Christology in this context, not in Part III. (*d*) Paul appears to have been more interested in the post-existence of Christ than in his pre-existence.

What Paul says about Christ's pre-existence is extremely limited. We already noted the idea that the pre-existent Christ was present with Israel in the wilderness (1 Cor. 10:1–5). Second-century writers like Justin emphasized Christ's role in the OT and in the experience of Israel because they understood the pre-existent Christ as the divine Logos (Word), virtually interchangeable with Sophia. But Paul himself does not develop this possibility in his letters. He may very well have done so in his preaching, however. In 1 Cor. 8:6 he assumes that what was said about Wisdom is true of Christ: "through whom are all things and through whom we exist." How Paul connected the role of the pre-existent Wisdom with the mission of Jesus is not clear; what is clear is that Paul did not regard Jesus as a wise man, or as a teacher of wisdom. It is remarkable that Paul seems not to have called Jesus Wisdom/Sophia. Even though 1 Cor. 1:24 actually refers to Christ as "the power of God and the wisdom of God," the term "wisdom" is not used in this technical sense.

Incarnation

What Paul says about the "incarnation" (a word he does not actually use) is rather diverse. Sometimes the subject of the verb is God: "God sent forth his Son, born of woman" (Gal. 4:4; see also Rom. 8:3); this "sending" does not refer to God's sending Jesus forth from the carpenter shop but to his sending the pre-existent one into time-space to become Jesus. Sometimes the subject of the verb is Christ himself, as in 2 Cor. 8:9 (see also Rom. 1:3; Phil. 2:6-7). As with the death of Christ, so the incarnation is spoken of either as an act of God or as an act of God's Son.

The most important christological passage is the hymn in Phil. 2:6-11, which Paul uses as a warrant for an ethical injunction (see the context in 2:3—4:12). The hymn itself is not concerned with ethics (the moral example of Jesus) but with the "shape" of the Son's career. No christological passage in Paul's letter has generated more discussion than this one. (Martin's *Carmen Christi* provides the best overview of the issues and the literature.) Only the most important aspects of this passage can be mentioned here. (*a*) Every translation must supply the verb in verse 5b, and whatever verb is supplied reveals a particular understanding of Paul's point. The RSV's "which you have in Christ Jesus" reveals the longstanding interpretation that the hymn celebrates "the mind of Christ." I prefer something like "which also you think in Christ" or "which also was embodied in Christ." (*b*) The phrases in vv. 7-8 mark the successive stages in the humiliation of the pre-existent one: Did not count equality with God a thing to be grasped (the RSV beautifully preserves the ambiguity of the Greek— "to be grasped" can mean either held onto or reached for), emptied himself, taking the form of a servant (or slave), being born (better, coming into existence) in the likeness of man, humbled himself and became obedient unto death. (It is widely believed that Paul inserted "even death on a cross.") (*c*) The turning point is at v. 9, where the exaltation (by resurrection) is mentioned.

Some exegetes, it should be noted, understand the hymn quite differently, because they see in the lines that characterize the downward movement of the Son toward death a conscious contrast between the obedience of the human Jesus and Adam's disobedience, thereby finding no reference to pre-existence whatever. Others see in "servant" an allusion to the Suffering Servant of Isaiah. We should not forget that this is a piece of poetry (though scholars disagree on how to apportion the lines into strophes), not a precise theological analysis; poetry highlights and celebrates, and deliberately sets up resonances with known motifs. Accordingly one must not read too much out of, or into, the passage.

For our immediate concern, it is important to see, first, that had Paul not agreed with this hymn he would not have quoted it. It must accord with

what he had preached about Christ to the Philippians. Second, the shape
of the incarnation is humiliation, weakness, and obedience—as 2 Cor. 8:9
also implies. Third, implicit in this passage is the view that no one could
have looked at Jesus and concluded, "There goes God in the flesh." Not
even the principalities and powers recognized him as the Lord of glory,
otherwise they would not have had him crucified (1 Cor. 2:8). Fourth, if
this passage puts us in touch with how Paul preached Christ, then it is clear
that his preaching had no place for the exorcism stories we find in Mark,
which report that the demonic powers recognized Jesus' true identity and
tried to defend themselves against his power (Mark 1:24). Indeed, it is
unlikely that Paul would have found any miracle stories about Jesus congenial to his gospel, for they all expressed the view that Jesus is a bearer
of divine power. For Paul, however, the career of Jesus was not marked by
power but by weakness and vulnerability, even to the point of death. It is
interesting to speculate on what sort of gospel Paul might have written.

Post-existence

What Paul says about the post-existent Son is also diverse. For con-
venience, we can cluster the references into two groups: First, Paul sometimes speaks of the present activity of the post-existent one, now the Lord.
Later theologians would have to cope with the ease with which Paul shifts
from statements about what Christ is now doing among the believers to
what the Spirit is doing (thus according to Rom. 8:34 Christ intercedes for
us before God, but in v. 26 it is the Spirit that does this). According to 2
Cor. 3:17 "the Lord is the Spirit." This sentence must not be reversed,
because for Paul the Spirit is not Lord but rather the Lord is present
through the Spirit and thereby remains sovereign precisely in what we
might call "religious experience." Because the Lord is actively at work (in,
with, or through the Spirit) among believers, Paul can give his exhortations
"in the Lord" (1 Thess. 4:1). The resurrection exalted Jesus and translated
him into a state of sovereignty and into a mode of being in which he is intimately related to everyone who believes and has the Spirit.

Second, Christ's own present status is transitional. According to 1 Cor.
15:24, Christ is now conqueror of hostile powers, including death (Rom.
14:9), but when this conquest is complete Christ's own status will change.
Thus Paul's understanding of Christ's post-existent work is governed by his
expectation of the Lord's return which Paul believed to be imminent. Here
too Paul uses a diverse vocabulary. He can call it the *parousia* (coming)

of the Son (1 Thess. 1:10), but usually he speaks of the coming of the Lord
(1 Thess. 2:19; 3:13; 4:15; 5:23; Phil. 4:5), and once of awaiting a savior
from heaven (Phil. 3:20). He can speak of God as the future judge (Rom.
2:16; 3:6), and he can also say that the judge will be Christ (2 Cor. 5:10;
see also 1 Cor. 4:5). He can allude to the future coming of the Lord
because it was a fixed part of his preaching, as he says in 1 Thess. 1:9–10.

What, then, was the "shape" of the pivotal event in Paul's preaching?
The event of Jesus was part of the career of God's Son which began before
creation and will end at the Parousia, when all things will be transformed
and God will be "all in all." The event of Jesus itself was characterized by
obedience, vulnerability, and weakness to the point of death, and was followed by exaltation to Lordship now being exercised in God's name until
the end. In other words, the event of Jesus derives its significance in part
from the fact that it is linked to the OT (Rom. 1:2), and in part from the
fact that it is seen in a mythic framework. Paul did not have to invent the
framework when he preached the gospel; it was already available in the cultural and religious heritage which he shared with his readers. New was the
way it was correlated with Jesus, whose historical life ended on the cross
but whose eschatological life began at resurrection. What made the event
good news was the insight that the cross occurred "for our sins," and that
the resurrection of Jesus was the prototype of our own transformation.

Having sketched the gospel that Paul preached, we turn next to explore
the redemptive response which Paul elicited from those who believed what
he had to say.

CHAPTER FOUR

THE SALVIFIC RESPONSE

In Paul's gospel, the message about Christ was one center of an ellipse; the other center was his hearers. That is, Paul's statements about God and Christ were always worked out vis-à-vis their significance for the human condition. What the gospel announces is not a set of assertions about God and Christ that one can acknowledge as true without having one's life changed. To put it more formally: Christology implies soteriology (the understanding of salvation), and vice versa.

The salvific significance of the Christ-event as proclaimed in the gospel was expressed in various ways by Paul. Each term highlighted a particular facet of the human condition and its appropriate resolution. For example, reconciliation implies that the human condition is alienation or hostility with respect to God; redemption is buying back, as when a person redeems his radio at a pawnshop. Other characteristic word-pictures include justification (being set in right relation), new creation, and adoption. Absent from Paul's vocabulary of salvation were forgiveness and new birth (or regeneration). The most comprehensive term was *sotēria* (salvation).

What Paul's gospel announced was not publicly manifest—that Christ died for our sins and was resurrected by God to be the Lord. Only the crucifixion was a public fact, but its soteriological meaning was inseparable from the resurrection. Therefore Paul's message was gospel, good news, only for the person who believed it. Consequently Paul, like every early Christian preacher, called for faith. Apart from faith, Paul's word brought no salvation. This is why the discussion of the response will consider first Paul's understanding of faith. Because those who believed what Paul said were baptized, the second section will consider Paul's interpretation of Christian baptism. Finally, we shall look at his understanding of the new community, *ekklēsia* (the church).

Faith as Trust

Faith as a personal decision and commitment was endemic to Christianity from the start, because one became a Christian by believing a message, not by being faithful to inherited religious beliefs and customs. This is why Christians were, and continue to be called "believers." Moreover, in Paul's day, all believers were converts—first-generation Christians. None of them had grown up in a Christian community; none became Christian by claiming the faith of the previous generation as his or her own. Furthermore, probably most of them had been "religious" in some sense, whether as members of a synagogue, as worshipers of civic gods, or as initiates of the mystery cults such as Isis and Osiris. Consequently, most persons came into Christianity with other notions about faith, sacraments, religious customs, and so forth. Paul's understanding of faith, itself rooted in Judaism but reshaped by his experience with the risen Christ, therefore had to maintain its identity and develop its profile in a complex setting which repeatedly threatened to distort it. (Paul's defense of faith and its adequacy is considered in Part III.)

For Paul faith is a response to a proclamation, a spoken word. Nothing could be farther from Paul than the popular notion that it does not matter so much what a person believes so long as one believes it sincerely enough and believes it fervently enough so that it "works." That makes faith a psychological state; salvation then results from success in believing, in cultivating and maintaining a disposition. That, in turn, would make salvation into an achievement, something attainable by anyone who attained a requisite intensity of faith. There is, of course, such a thing as the dynamics of faith, just as there are patterns and processes (describable psychologically) by which one comes to faith and lives by it, but Paul was not interested in describing them or in reflecting on them. His concern was theological.

Romans 10:17 is basic, though difficult to translate adequately. The RSV has, "So faith comes from what is heard, and what is heard comes from the preaching of Christ." The NEB has, "faith is awakened by the message, and the message that awakens it comes through the word of Christ." "The preaching of Christ" (RSV) or "the word of Christ" (NEB) does not mean Christ's own preaching; rather, it means the message whose content is Christ. Moreover, it is not certain that both the NEB's "awakened by the message" and the RSV's "faith comes from what is heard" render adequately what Paul literally wrote: "Faith comes from *akoē*"—a word that can mean "hearing" as well as the "thing heard." In any case, this accent on hearing a message as the event that awakens faith is central to Paul. It is not reducible to hearing sermons, nor simply equatable with oral communication, though it embraces both.

Three aspects of this "hearing" need to be noted.

(a) Faith is a response, not an inference, deduction, or value judgment on a body of information—though it may include these. Neither an inference, nor a deduction, nor a value judgment is good news *for* the self because these processes are acts initiated *by* the self. From Paul's angle, the self that needs salvation can no more generate its own salvation than a psychotic can become his or her own therapist. The self needing salvation must be accosted by a word that creates an alternative and calls for a response. Paul's word for that response is *pistis* (usually translated "faith").

(b) Hearing implies that the gospel must be articulated. A deed of love or compassion can embody it, but a deed remains ambiguous apart from interpretation. For example, Jesus' exorcisms embodied his message, but they were interpreted as evidence that he was in league with the devil (Mark 3:22). Therefore, for Paul the crucifixion was gospel only if it were presented not as the story of a martyr for a cause, but as God's act, as an event for our sins. Only if the meaning of the Christ-event is articulated for the human dilemma can one respond to it appropriately.

(c) The response that is appropriate to hearing is heeding. Paul himself connected *akoē* (hearing) with *hypakoē* (heeding, obeying), for he understood faith as obedience. When he mentioned the Thessalonians' coming to faith, he wrote of their "obedience" (1 Thess. 1:8); in Rom. 1:8 he wrote of "your faith" and in Rom. 16:19 of "your faith," clearly meaning the same thing. In Rom. 1:5 he actually used the phrase, "obedience of faith," probably meaning "obedience which is faith," for Rom. 10:16 refers to those who have rejected the gospel as not "obeying" it, not heeding what they heard, not responding with *pistis*. How does one "obey" good news?

When Paul understands faith as obedience, he does not regard the gospel as a command. Rather, it is a message that makes a claim on the hearer, one which calls for a response that has a moral quality to it, not merely an intellectual assent. This moral quality of the response shows that faith is trust, for trust is a moral act. It energizes the will no less than the mind or feelings; trust is a response of the whole self. When that response is to a word that makes a claim on the hearer, that response can be called obedience.

Trust is a useful way of expressing what Paul means by *pistis*. Indeed, the passive verb of the same root word is normally translated "entrusted with" (Rom. 3:2; Gal. 2:7; 1 Thess. 2:4; 1 Tim. 1:11; Titus 1:3). "Trust" is both a verb and a noun, but we have no verbal form for "faith" (we cannot say, "She faiths") but must shift to "believe." But "believe" also creates difficulties, for its opposite is to disbelieve, and sometimes doubt. Moreover, because "believe" is often associated with "beliefs" it is easy to slip into understanding faith primarily as believing beliefs (assenting to doctrines). Actually, the response Paul sought included both consent to the truth of his statements about God's act in Christ and personal entrustment of the self to the God who had done this and to Christ.

To trust is to commit oneself. To trust a person is to rely on that person and to allow oneself to be shaped by that person on a deep level, for the object of trust shapes the truster. To trust a message is to rely on it, to act on it, to be shaped by it. The more radical the message, the deeper the response. In fact, who we are is determined by whom and what we trust (or distrust), by what we count on. Our identity is constituted by the pattern or network of trusts, the configuration of that to which we are committed because we deem it trustworthy. That in which all our trusts are finally grounded is what we call "God," and functions as "God" even if one is not explicitly or constantly "religious."

When Paul called for trust, then, he was calling for reconfiguration of the self. To trust God as presented in the message of the cross/resurrection and of Jesus' Lordship and coming is to challenge the previous configurations of trust and their ground. If one rejects the gospel, then one maintains the status quo. If one accepts the message, then one begins to realign that configuration—one heeds the message, "obeys" the gospel. If the message were a command, a law, this response might be compliance, not obedience. But for Paul, the message is a word about what God has done for humanity while it was still enmeshed in false commitments (in sin): "While we were yet sinners, Christ died for us" (Rom. 5:8). That is, it is a message about an act of God's grace. The only way one can heed the news of God's grace is to entrust oneself to this God.

Faith/trust is also confession, deliberate avowal. For Paul, trust is genuinely Christian only when it is directed toward someone or something outside the self—God, the gospel, and the Christ it announces. Were this not the case, Paul would have faith in faith; he would trust the power of trusting. That would make the realignment of trusts depend on the intensity of trust. One would end up trying to "believe harder"; those who believed best would be most saved. Moreover, because the gospel is spoken to persons who already have a network of trusts, it does not reach them as neutrals but as persons whose lives already embody commitments, tacit or explicit. To trust the gospel therefore calls for a deliberate decision, an act of avowal, a confession. Calling Christians "believers" is really shorthand, for they are not persons who major in believing. Rather, they are persons who believe what the gospel says and whom it proclaims, and who entrust themselves to it deliberately.

This intimate relationship between trusting and confessing is made explicit in Rom. 10:9, where Paul uses traditional language probably associated with baptism: "If you confess with your lips that Jesus is Lord and believe in your heart that God raised him from the dead, you will be saved." This sentence is laced into a complex interpretation of Deuteronomy 30. Paul's exegetical method is like that used at Qumran, the so-called midrash-pesher method. A line of Scripture is quoted, followed by a statement of its current meaning, "this is . . . " Deut. 30:14, referring to the Torah, reads, "The word is near you, in your mouth and in your heart." Paul says that this is the "word of faith which we preach"—the message that calls for a self-entrusting response. The carefully balanced sentence shows that Paul is writing about a single act:

| confess | mouth | Jesus is Lord | righteousness |
| believe | heart | resurrection | salvation |

To confess is to acknowledge that the stated content is both true and "true for me." To confess Jesus as Lord is to avow that he has an ultimate claim on my life and that this claim is valid because of what God had done through him. To believe the resurrection with the heart is to believe it with one's will and emotions; it is a matter of commitment and trust.

In the foregoing verse Paul identified that toward which confession and trust are directed as assertions of fact; he used traditional formulations introduced by "that": "that Jesus is Lord," and so forth (see also 1 Thess. 4:14). But sometimes Paul also speaks of trust in Christ, and uses a variety of expressions to do so. These are commonly rendered by the same phrase, "faith in Christ." For example, in Phil. 1:29 and Gal. 2:16 Paul writes of believing *eis auton* (toward, unto, *in* him). In Rom. 10:11, using the LXX, he writes of believing *on* him (*ep' autō*). Thus another question emerges: What is the relation between trust directed to a statement ("that . . . ") and trust directed toward a person, Christ?

It is easy to overemphasize the difference between the two. For Paul there is no substantial difference between personal trust in Jesus Christ and trust/faith directed toward gospel-statements about God's deed in Christ, for the Christ whom Paul trusts is identical with the Christ announced in the "that . . . " statements.

Because Paul understood trust to be the sole condition for being rightly related to God, he saw that Gentiles need not become Jews in order to be valid Christians. He found support for this in the Scripture itself: "No one who believes in him will be put to shame" (Rom. 10:11, quoting Isa. 28:16). Paul took this at face value: If no one believes in vain, then everyone who believes/trusts is saved. So he continues, "For there is no distinction between Jew and Greek [Gentile]; the same Lord is Lord of all and bestows his riches upon all who call upon him [= make the confession], for 'everyone who calls upon the name of the Lord will be saved' " (Rom. 10:12–13, quoting Joel 2:32).

One should take note of the import of Paul's understanding of trust for his mission. In the first place, if one is rightly related to God by trusting him, then this relation is available to every person as a person, as a self. One does not need to become a Jewish self, or a sophisticated self, or any other kind of self in order to qualify. Rather, it is precisely as a human self that one can trust God on the basis of the gospel. In other words, Paul broke through all categories and divisions that classified people into groups and social strata. He laid hold of the rudimentary, constitutive factor in every self—the network of trusts that makes a self what it is. This is why he could say, "There is neither Jew nor Greek, there is neither slave nor free, there is neither male nor female; for you are all one in Christ" (Gal. 3:28). Of course Paul knew that these distinctions still existed. But they no longer determined who one really is before God, nor decisively modified the right relation to God which is trust. Every self that trusts God on the basis of the gospel is rightly related to its ground.

In the second place, Paul broke through to the corresponding fundamental meaning of "God." In Rom. 3:29–30, Paul appeals precisely to the core doctrine of Judaism—that "God is one"—to argue that "God is not God of Jews only." Just as there is "neither Jew nor Greek" person before God but only persons, so there is neither "Jewish God" nor "Greek God" who deals with persons. Rather, the one God rectifies the one situation in which all persons find themselves, and does so by means of one relationship— trust. Paul did not achieve this remarkable clarity by asserting the innate goodness of all persons, nor by appealing to the spark of divinity in every self, but by uncovering the solidarity of all persons in bondage to sin. That theme will concern us in Part III. Now, however, we will turn to that event which marked the entry of Jew and Gentile into a new community—baptism.

Baptism into Christ

How Paul presented baptism in connection with his preaching the gospel is rather elusive. In 1 Cor. 1:14–17 it is implied that he did not make baptism crucial to his mission. Because he nonetheless assumes that his Christian readers have all been baptized, it is clear that baptism was part of Paul's mission. Moreover, Paul repeatedly made baptism the basis on which he built an argument, thereby showing that it was a fundamental component of the response he sought for his preaching. Still, 1 Cor. 1:14–17 shows that Paul did not know the tradition in Matt. 28:16–20, according to which the risen Jesus not only commissioned the apostles to baptize but also specified the formula they were to use.

In order to understand how Paul may have presented baptism to his converts, it is necessary to combine what little we know about early Christian baptism with what we can infer from what Paul assumes in his letters.

Several things can be said about early Christian baptism in Paul's time. (a) Baptism was not invented by Christians nor derived from Jesus' own mission. Yet Christians began baptizing those who accepted their message. It is not known whether they derived this practice from John the Baptist's precedent, or precisely how they interpreted it. (b) Baptism functioned as a rite that marked entry into the Christian community. (c) The rite itself was apparently by immersion. The occasion was marked by an act of confession and administered "in the name of Jesus" (Acts 2:38; 1 Cor. 1:13; the triune formula in Matt. 28:19 was developed later). (d) The problem of whether to baptize infants of Christian parents did not arise in Paul's time. Then, it was those who confessed Jesus as Lord (and their households, according to Acts 16:15) who were baptized. (e) It is highly unlikely that any Christian would have regarded baptism as "only a symbol," as an action whose main importance lay in what is signified "outside" the action itself. Rather, for the ancients in general, rites actually did something; the action had power. In other words, it is likely that early Christians regarded baptism as a sacramental act. (f) Early Christians assumed that the gift of the Holy Spirit was linked with baptism, that every baptized person received the Spirit.

It is not unusual for religious rites to be performed in much the same way while receiving new and different interpretations. In this light, we may assume that the Pauline mission practiced baptism in accord with these common understandings, while at the same time understood the rite in a new way—as an act that made one a participant in Christ's death. It is unlikely that this interpretation had been developed in Palestinian Jewish Christianity. Was it then original with Paul? Apparently not, for he asked the Roman readers who had not yet heard him preach, "Do you not know that all of us who have been baptized into Christ Jesus were baptized into his death?" (Rom. 6:3). He assumes that they—Hellenistic Jewish and Hellenistic gentile Christians—share his view that baptism is "baptism into Christ."

Such an understanding of baptism is possible only if "Christ" is understood in a particular way. In Rom. 5:12–21, Paul had contrasted Adam and Christ, not simply as individuals but also as "corporate persons"—persons who, without losing their individuality, included others. It is exceedingly difficult to conceptualize this because our thinking is profoundly individualistic. The "social contract" view of society and of government allows us to think of isolates deliberately forming aggregates, but inhibits us from thinking of actual participation in a single person "at the head of the line." Something of an analogy may be useful, however. Blacks often sensed that what happened to Martin Luther King, Jr., was happening to them as well. When he was at the White House, they were there; when he was shot, they were shot. This analogy may be suggestive, but it also has clear limits, for Dr. King was a symbolic representative of the whole. For Paul, however, Christ and Adam were more than representative figures, ones who "stood for" a group. They embodied the group and determined its fundamental character.

Baptism "into Christ" was a rite by which one became a participant in Christ, the inclusive Man (person, not male!), the new Adam (a phrase Paul does not actually use). This participation in Christ was not a "mystical experience" of conscious identification or absorption into Christ. The accent was not on consciousness at all or on "religious experience" but rather on the "objective" transference into a domain of power. To be baptized into Christ is to be included in the domain of Christ, his field of force.

The same understanding lies behind the rather complex passage in Galatians 3, where Paul argues that the promise to Abraham is fulfilled in Christ. Paul notes (Gal. 3:16) that Gen. 12:7 mentions Abraham's "seed" (i.e., offspring), and that the noun is singular. So Paul concludes that the offspring of Abraham to which Genesis refers is Christ. At the end of the chapter Paul says "in Christ Jesus you are all sons of God, through faith" (Gal. 3:26). Because whoever has been baptized into Christ has "put on" Christ, now there is neither Jew nor Greek, slave nor free, male nor female, "for you are all one in Christ Jesus. And if you are Christ's you are Abraham's offspring. . . . " Paul reasons this way because he believes baptism actually makes a person participate in Christ.

Paul shared with Hellenistic Christianity the interpretation of baptism as a rite which made one a participant in Christ, but his own emphasis concerned the center of "Christ"—the cross and resurrection. Paul never says that the baptized participate in Christ's post-existent glory, let alone his divinity. Rather, in keeping with his focus on the cross, he says that those who were baptized were "baptized into his death" (Rom. 6:3). In other words, this phrase specified how "baptism into Christ" is to be understood. Paul's phrase "buried with him through baptism into death" is the heart of the matter. Romans 6:1-11 is characterized by expressions which we must render as "being X with Christ"—buried with him (v. 4); planted together, that is, grown together (RSV: united with, v. 5); crucified with (v. 6); die with (v. 8); live with (v. 8). What is in view is not an empathetic state but a sacramental act which actually united the baptizand with Christ. Paul does not mean that baptism somehow makes the past event of Christ present to the individual. It is rather the other way around: the individual is made a participant in Christ's death.

It is important to note that although Paul insists that the baptizand participates in Christ's death, Paul *never* says that one also participates in Christ's resurrection by baptism. In Rom. 6:8 we read, "But if we have died with Christ [as indeed we have] we believe that we *shall* also live with him." Participation in Christ's resurrection is future. One reason the Letters to the Colossians and Ephesians are considered to be deutero-Pauline is that they regard participation in Christ's resurrection as something already experienced (Col. 3:1; Eph. 1:20). In Rom. 6:4, on the other hand, we read, "We were buried . . . with him . . . so that *as* Christ was raised from the dead . . . we too might walk in newness of life." In short, Christ's resurrection is the basis of a new moral life; the actual resurrection of the Christian awaits the Parousia.

Apparently the Corinthian Christians did infer that already they participated also in Christ's resurrection and that this gave them a measure of invulnerability in the world (i.e., they were sacramental enthusiasts). To counter this, Paul compares the post-baptismal Christians with Israel in the wilderness, even saying that the latter had been "baptized into Moses" when they went through the sea; yet they did not reach Canaan because their "post-baptismal sin" was so great that they were destroyed (1 Cor. 10:1-13). Paul's "consider yourselves dead to sin and alive to God in Christ Jesus" (Rom. 6:11) means that the baptized are to claim now the new life of the future resurrection, but to do so as a warrant for a new ethic. This is why Paul's exhortations can be grounded in baptism (see 1 Cor. 6:9-11).

The New Community

Just as Paul both shared the early Christian understanding of baptism and developed his own accent, so he shared certain understandings of the church and at the same time contributed his own emphasis—the body of Christ.

Paul's letters use traditional terms for the Christian community without explaining them. This shows that he had already introduced this terminology as part of his teaching. One of these terms is "saints" (Rom. 8:27; 12:13; 15:25, 26; 16:2; 1 Cor. 6:1; 16:1; Phil. 1:4; 4:22). Basically "saints" are not particularly holy persons who stand out from the rest by their unusual spirituality. Paul would have repudiated anyone singling him out as "St. Paul," just as he would have refused to call Peter "St. Peter." Every Christian is a saint, a person made holy (sanctified) by the presence of God's holy Spirit. In this light, the RSV's translation of Rom. 1:7 and 1 Cor. 1:2 is misleading if not plainly wrong: "called to be saints." Sainthood is not a goal toward which the believer is invited. Rather, it should be translated "called saints"; Christians are, by definition, "called." "Called saints" does not mean "labeled 'saints' " (as in "the people called 'Methodists' "). Rather, "called" refers to God's sovereign act of including these persons in the People of God. ("Saints" is an OT term for the elect people, especially the eschatological People of God.) Paul addressed gentile Christians as "saints" because he regarded them as part of the eschatological People of God, "the Israel of God" (Gal. 6:16).

A second term for the community which was not peculiar to Paul is *ekklēsia,* commonly translated "church." In the LXX *ekklēsia* translates *qahal,* assembly or congregation. For Paul *ekklēsia* usually refers to the local congregation (1 Thess. 1:1), as the plural shows (1 Cor. 11:16; Gal. 1:2; 2 Cor. 8:1). But it can also be used of the Christian community as a whole, for when 1 Cor. 12:28 says "God has appointed in the church first apostles," and so forth, Paul clearly has more in view than the Corinthian congregation. (See also 1 Cor. 15:9.)

Paul's understanding of the church manifests itself throughout his letters. Indeed, one can say that his entire letter-writing activity is his struggle for a right understanding of what it means for Christians to be church. This is apparent not only in his rather stringent discipline (e.g., 1 Cor. 5:1—6:11), but also in his concern for the moral life of Christians (e.g., Romans 12—13), for order in worship (1 Corinthians 12—14), and for internal harmony (Phil. 2:1-4; 4:2-3). What enhances the community ("builds up," "edifies") is prominent in the warrants Paul adduces for his moral appeals (e.g., 1 Cor. 14:2-4; 1 Thess. 5:11).

On the other hand, Paul's letters show only slight interest in providing the readers with a correct doctrine of the church, an ecclesiology; nor do they show any concern for questions of church polity (proper organization). Rather, in Paul's small house-church congregations diverse roles were regarded as manifestations of the diverse gifts of the Spirit, as 1 Corinthians 12 shows. This fluidity in leadership roles is one of the things that distinguished Paul's own understanding of the church from what the author of Ephesians wrote in Paul's name. In Eph. 4:7-12, the writer regards distinct offices of the church as gifts of the Spirit, whereas Paul wrote of roles and capacities to function in particular ways (1 Cor. 12:4-11). Moreover, in Ephesians the church itself has become the subject matter of theological reflection—in fact, the church is now God's destined answer to the problem of the cosmos because it is the body of Christ.

"Body of Christ" may well have been Paul's own distinctive contribution to the community's self-understanding. Ephesians and Colossians developed this beyond Paul; the undisputed letters never *describe* the church as the body of Christ in so many words (as do Eph. 1:22-23; Col. 1:18). Instead Paul *addresses* the readers, "you are the body of Christ" (1 Cor. 12:27), and he does so as a warrant for an exhortation to unity.

The metaphor of a body with diverse organs was known also in popular Stoicism. In this vein Paul *compares* the church with a body in 1 Cor. 12:12-26. But when he *identifies* the readers as the body of Christ (1 Cor. 12:27) he moves beyond metaphor toward myth—the myth of a cosmic body constituted by Christians. The extent to which this identification reflects a gnostic myth of the cosmic redeemer, whose body consists of the saved, is disputed. C. K. Barrett (*The First Epistle to the Corinthians*, 292), for instance, says that the genitive is "not of identity but of possession"—not the body which is Christ but the body that belongs to Christ. Yet 1 Cor. 12:13 writes of being "baptized into one body," suggesting that somehow the body of Christ is a transcendent entity, not simply an earthly community. In the last analysis, it is less than clear exactly how Paul thought of "the body of Christ."

Paul's understanding of the Christian community is disclosed not only in what he said about it and to it, but also in what he said about its rites. We have already commented on baptism; now we turn to the Lord's Supper.

Probably this was the high point of worship; it is equally probable that this occurred on Sundays (1 Cor. 16:1). Moreover, the Lord's Supper was not separated from the church supper. This separation actually began with Paul's advice to the Corinthians (1 Cor. 11:17–34, esp. v. 34). The fact that the Lord's Supper was part of the church supper was one of the things that made the crisis in Antioch so severe, for when Jewish Christians withdrew from the common table they also withdrew from the communion table (Gal. 2:11–13).

How Paul interpreted the Lord's Supper when he introduced it to his churches must be inferred from the tradition which he taught (1 Cor. 11:23–25) and from 1 Cor. 10:16–17 where he reminds them of what the meal means in order to make another point.

The Lord's Supper tradition in 1 Corinthians 11 is the oldest written form of the tradition, antedating Mark by fifteen or more years. But Mark's form of the tradition (Mark 12:22–25) is often regarded as essentially older, less Hellenistic, than Paul's (probably developed at Antioch).

Two features call for a comment: (*a*) The Lord's Supper tradition celebrates what the other piece of tradition reports—that "Christ died for our sins" (1 Cor. 15:3). This manifests itself in the phrasing. Not only does the tradition begin with "on the night when he was handed over," but the language makes more explicit what is implied in Mark:

Mark: This is my body.
Paul: This is my body which is for you (some MSS: broken for you).
Mark: This is my blood of the covenant (some MSS: new covenant) which is
      poured out for many.
Paul: This is the new covenant in my blood.

Thus Paul's tradition explicitly extends the atonement theme to the bread. Paul's tradition also recasts the covenant motif in order to make explicit the claim that Jer. 31:31 is now a reality. (*b*) Paul's tradition includes the com mand to repeat the rite "in remembrance" of Christ, a motif absent from Mark (but present in the longer form of the text in Luke). This remembrance is more than recollection; it has to do with commemoration, an act in which the meaning of the past is made present. It does not suggest that Christ's death is repeated ritually.

In 1 Cor. 10:16–17 we read the word "communion" for the Supper. Here Paul reminds the Corinthians that the cup and the bread (the reversed sequence does not reveal a different tradition) are "communion" (*koinōnia*) in the blood of Christ. By drinking and eating the congregation shares in Christ. Because the Corinthians understand this, Paul could appeal: You cannot eat the Lord's Supper and participate in a sacred meal at local shrines as well because this ritual eating makes one a participant in the reality being celebrated (1 Cor. 10:20–21).

It was just this understanding of sacral and sacramental eating/drinking which led to a development that Paul regarded as gross distortion. Precisely what was going on and what the Corinthians thought they were doing continues to be debated. Nonetheless, it is reasonably clear that they understood the Supper in a highly sacramental way. To imagine what was going on, we must recall that the group met in a home of a wealthier Christian whose dwelling could accommodate the group. Moreover, since there was neither a "legal Sunday" nor a standard quitting time from work, there was probably no fixed "church hour" either. People came when they could, and the gatherings may well have lasted for hours, perhaps far into the night (if Acts 20:7 is a clue). Apparently those who arrived first began eating and drinking, so that by the time everyone had arrived, some had already had too much (1 Cor. 11:21). Moreover, the poor were humiliated by the little they brought (v. 22). The Corinthians saw no reason to share with each other or to wait for one another because they understood the religious meaning of eating and drinking as participation in the Lord, apparently emphasizing participation in the risen Lord's power and Spirit. The communing was between the individual and the Lord; what difference did it make who else was or was not there?

The Corinthian abuse of the Supper shows how ritual, socioeconomic, and theological issues were intertwined. Gerd Theissen has analyzed the Corinthian situation suggestively. (See his "Social Integration and Sacramental Activity: An Analysis of 1 Cor. 11:17–34," in *The Social Setting of Pauline Christianity*, 145–74).

Paul does not hesitate to say, "When you meet together, it is not the

Lord's Supper (*kyriakon deipnon*) that you eat." They certainly thought it was! How then can Paul make such a statement? Because, first, this participation is not primarily in the power and glory of the risen Lord but in his death. This is why he repeats the tradition, and adds his comment: "For as often as you eat this bread and drink this cup, you proclaim the Lord's death until he comes." Second, he goes on to write about "discerning the Lord's body" (1 Cor. 11:29). When he adds that sickness (and even death) has befallen those who participated "unworthily" he shows that he too regards the meal as a sacrament with power which, if abused, brings a curse instead of a blessing. At the same time, the entire context shows that the body of Christ which is to be "discerned" in the occasion is not merely the bread, but also the church. One may even infer that for Paul the body of Christ is not only *on* the table but also *at* the table since 1 Cor. 10:16–17 explicitly connects the two: "The bread which we break, is it not a participation in the body of Christ? Because there is one loaf, we who are many are one body, for we all partake of the same loaf."

Thus Paul understands the Supper as a sacramental rite which involves the believers not only with Christ, specifically with his death, but also with one another. The unity of the community is not the result of mutual accommodation, a social contract, but the result of being "baptized into one body" and of eating one loaf. Therefore, "if one member suffers, all suffer together; if one member is honored, all rejoice together" (1 Cor. 12:26). What was happening in Corinth was just the opposite. Therefore their meals were not "the Lord's Supper," regardless of how the Corinthians may have understood it and irrespective of how "meaningful" their experiences might have been.

CHAPTER FIVE

THE DEEPER LOGIC OF PAUL'S GOSPEL

The interpreter of Paul meets not only specific concepts, such as grace, law, or Spirit, but also a way of thinking which may seem strange. Grasping Paul's thought therefore requires more than clarifying a group of concepts. It also calls for understanding the perspective within which these concepts function, the deeper logic that gives coherence to his thought.

Because Paul's letters are not treatises in theology but pastoral letters occasioned by particular problems, he did not identify his governing assumptions; nor did he usually indicate the logical connections between them. Ascertaining the deeper coherence of this thought therefore entails certain risks. One may unwittingly impose one's own sense of coherence on Paul; one may also end up making Paul more systematic than he really was. Nonetheless, the risk is worth taking.

In getting at the deeper logic of his gospel, we will focus on three motifs or perspectives rather than on "doctrines": the sovereign freedom of God; creation and new creation; and participation and anticipation. We are not interested here in detecting the origin of these motifs, or in calling attention to the mythic factor in them, but in perceiving their inner theological coherence. Gaining some clarity here will help us understand how Paul deepened certain theological emphases in his letters (Part III).

The Sovereign Freedom of God

Fundamental to Paul's understanding and interpretation of God is the conviction that God's activity manifests his sovereign freedom to be faithful to himself and to his commitments. This understanding of God was deeply rooted in the OT and in Judaism. Nonetheless, the gospel Paul preached induced him to rethink this motif and to express it, especially in Romans, in several characteristically Pauline ways. As already noted, it is likely that his own experience of being transformed from a persecutor into a propagator of the gospel radicalized his inherited understanding of God's sovereign freedom. Implicit in his conversion is the radical freedom of God vis-à-vis Paul's life, for his conversion implied that God was not bound to the way Paul was thinking of God or relating to God. Rather, God intervened in his life despite Paul. The logic of this experience implies that a God who is not free to do this cannot do anything decisive about the human situation; conversely, a God who has done this is disclosed as a radically free sovereign committed to setting things right. A God who is not free is reduced to a logarithmic function of culture, of nature's processes, or to the invisible coefficient of human achievement or consciousness. Such a God no longer stands over against culture or humanity with an identity of his own, but is reduced to the guarantor and ground of what is.

It is convenient to probe this motif by considering two polarities: (1) intentionality and achievement; and (2) newness and constancy. Although it was polemical and apologetic situations that elicited Paul's discussions of these themes, they were so fundamental to his gospel that it is appropriate to deal with them here.

Intentionality and Achievement

It is axiomatic for Paul that God has an intent, a will, a goal. Paul's understanding of God is telic (with a view toward the *telos*, end). For Paul, God is not a passive reality, but an intensely active one. Nor is Paul's God a remote divine watchmaker of the eighteenth-century Deists, the Creator who retired after constructing a law-abiding universe. Rather, Paul assumed that God is actively at work in pursuit of his goal. As we shall see, that goal embraces the redemption of creation. At the same time, Paul's letters contain no description of that goal. Nonetheless, his theology is more oriented toward the future than the past, more toward destiny than toward origins. This is because Paul understands himself to be living at the hinge of history, at the dawn of the New Age.

Though Paul's thinking embraces all creation, his letters contain remarkably little about his world view. Paul does not try to stand outside the world in order to see it as a whole. Rather, he locates himself in a particular place and lifts his eyes to the widest horizon from where he stands, namely, in the vortex where the gospel encountered him as a devout Jew. When Paul thinks about God's purpose he inevitably thinks in terms of Jews and Gentiles, and of Israel's role in God's purpose. He does not think abstractly about humanity (for which he has no word), nor about the self (he says virtually nothing about the nature of the soul).

As a matter of fact, Paul says very little about Israel's vocation in light of God's intentionality. What he does say in Rom. 2:17–29 does not celebrate the Jews' vocation but is actually an indictment of them. He picks up the catchwords of Jewish self-understanding (as he perceives it): "a guide to the blind, a light to those who are in darkness, a corrector of the foolish, a teacher of children, having in the law the embodiment of knowledge and truth." But he juxtaposes this with a list of accusations in order to conclude, " 'the name of God is blasphemed among the Gentiles because of you' " (quoting Isa. 52:5). Nonetheless, the prerogatives of the Jews vis-à-vis the Gentiles are affirmed: "They are Israelites, and to them belong the sonship, the glory, the covenants, the giving of the law, the worship, and the promises; to them belong the patriarchs and of their race, according to the flesh, is the Christ" (Rom. 9:4–5).

At this point it is appropriate to ask how Paul understands salvation history in light of the intentionality of God. The term "salvation history" has a checkered history in nineteenth- and twentieth-century theology. After World War II, Oscar Cullmann's book *Christ and Time* made it prominent especially in those Protestant circles unwilling to follow Rudolf Bultmann's existentialist interpretation. Subsequently it became prominent also in Catholic theology, partly because it introduced a dynamic element into biblical theology and thereby freed the Bible from being used primarily to provide proof texts for dogmatics. OT study, of course, evoked the theme in the first place because there was an emerging awareness that the history of Israel as reconstructed by critical historiography differed significantly from the way the OT itself told the story.

Salvation history is one translation of *Heilsgeschichte,* sometimes rendered as "history of salvation": the view that the bulk of the OT (apart from the Wisdom material) regards the individual stories, events, and epochs as "the line of God's action in the events of world history, which leads to the achievement of his purpose of the salvation of mankind" (Alan Richardson, *IDB* 4, 171).

"Salvation history" has made it possible for interpreters to do several things: (*a*) to give a green light to critical historiography concerning the individual items in the overall story; (*b*) to discern a theological unity in the diverse material; (*c*) to relate the OT to the NT. Thus Richardson continues: "It was by a particular series of historical events, through a particular national history, that God's saving purpose in Jesus Christ was fulfilled. It is because salvation is in the name of Jesus . . . that the biblical history is 'salvation history'; and it is for this reason that the salvation story is the story of Abraham . . . Moses . . . Rahab the harlot . . . David . . . and the prophets . . . and not the story of Buddha, Confucius, Socrates, Mohammed, Rousseau . . . " (ibid.). Pervading all the variations of salvation history is the view that the OT is a saga of God's dealing with Israel, leading up to Christ—at least in the Christian view of things.

Paul was often called as a chief witness on behalf of this theology. He certainly believed that God's intent came to decisive fulfillment in Christ. But can we say that he understood God's intent in terms of salvation *history*? Hardly! Unless we immediately add that he radically transformed the idea the way he (and his predecessors) transformed "Messiah" into Christ—that is, the office of a national redeemer-liberator was made into a personal name. True, the sample of Paul's preaching to the Hellenistic synagogue in Acts 13:16–41 does have Paul express a salvation history theology. It begins with the patriarchs, then mentions Exodus (omitting Sinai!), the conquest of Canaan, and highlights of the history up to David; then it moves to John the Baptist and the Jesus story. But Paul's letters give no indication that he actually preached this way. He did not read the Bible as a holy history; rather, in Rom. 3:2 he calls it "the oracles of God." To be sure, he appeals to some of the events mentioned in Acts 13, but he never discusses them as a sequence that constitutes a salvation history. For Paul the intentionality of God does not work itself out through Israel's history which culminates in Christ. The Christ-event, instead of being the capstone of a development, is a lens through which Paul sees the intent of God in a particular way.

The main place where Paul's understanding differs from that of salvation history is Romans 4, where he interprets Abraham. Paul adduces Abraham in support of his contention in Rom. 3:30—that since God is one, "he will justify the circumcised [the Jews] on the ground of their faith and the uncircumcised [the Gentiles] because of their faith." For both groups the right relation to God depends on the same thing—sheer trust.

Paul knows that God pronounced Abraham to be righteous in Gen. 15:6, and that the story of Abraham's circumcision is found in Genesis 17. Therefore God's gift of righteousness did not depend on circumcision. Hence circumcision was "a sign or seal of the righteousness which he had by faith when he was still uncircumcised" (v. 11). That is its meaning for Abraham; another meaning has to do with God's purpose. In Rom. 4:17 Paul appeals to Genesis 17, where God renewed the promise before Abraham circum

cised himself. The promise includes the statement, "I have made you the
father of many nations." With his eye on this statement, Paul asserts that
the purpose of Abraham's circumcision was to make him (a) "the father
of all who believe *without* being circumcised and who thus have righteousness reckoned to them" on the basis of faith, and likewise (b) "the father of
the circumcised who are not merely circumcised but also follow the example of the faith which our father Abraham had *before* he was circumcised"
(vv. 11–12). Thus Abraham is the father of all those whose relation to God
is a matter of trust. Paul implicitly denies that Abraham is the father of all
circumcised Jews, for he is truly father only of those who live by trust.

In Rom. 4:17b–22 Paul returns to Genesis 15 and interprets Abraham's
faith as sheer trust in the face of the evidence (i.e., lack of evidence): he
and Sarah were too old to have a child. Of Abraham Paul writes, "No distrust made him waver concerning the promise of God, but he grew strong
in his faith as he gave glory to God, fully convinced that God was able to
do what he had promised. That is why his faith 'was reckoned to him as
righteousness' " (Gen. 15:6). Why be concerned about Abraham's faith?
Because what was said of him was "written not for his sake alone but for
ours also." What God did in his case will be done in the case of Christians
also: trust "will be reckoned to us who believe in him that raised from the
dead Jesus our Lord. . . . " In other words, whoever believes the gospel
repeats Abraham's faith (v. 12) because Abraham too believed in the God
"who gives life to the dead [a double allusion to the deadness of Abraham's
virility and of Sarah's fecundity on the one hand and to God's resurrecting
Jesus on the other] and calls into existence the things that do not exist" (v.
17). The believers do not believe like Abraham (as v. 12 might imply);
rather they "share the faith of Abraham" (v. 16). This means that Christian
trust and Abrahamic trust are congruent; the structure of his trust in God
is identical with Christian trust in God. The trust of the Christian recapitu-
lates the trust of Abraham, the prototype of everyone who is justified by
faith.

Whatever one might think of Paul's exegesis, one thing at least should
be clear: he does not see the relation between the gospel and Abraham as
one of salvation *history,* for the gospel is not the culmination of what was
begun in Abraham but a recovery and actualization of it. As Paul said in
Gal. 3:8–9, "Scripture, foreseeing that God would justify the Gentiles by
faith, preached the gospel beforehand to Abraham, saying 'In thee shall all
the nations be blessed' " (Gen. 12:3). Consequently, those who believe

"are blessed with Abraham who had faith." God's intent for Abraham is not achieved in the history of Israel but in the existence of a community of Jews and Gentiles whose trust in God is Abrahamic.

Having looked at how Paul understands God's intentionality, we turn now to the other aspects of this first polarity, achievement. How does the sovereign freedom of God to achieve his intent manifest itself? One can argue that God achieves the intent for the Gentiles when they become Abraham's children by sheer trust; but how can one say that God's intent for Jews is being fulfilled when most Jews were in fact rejecting the gospel? What can Paul say about the frustration of God's intention?

Two possibilities are excluded: (*a*) God responds by rejecting the chosen people (Rom. 11:1); (*b*) God's word has "failed" (Rom. 9:6; NEB: has proved false). In rejecting the latter possibility Paul shows how he understands the sovereign freedom of God. In other words, what is commonly regarded as Paul's doctrine of election and predestination is really his exposition of God's sovereign freedom to achieve the divine purpose ultimately (Romans 9—11). It will repay us to look more closely at these chapters.

Paul's premise is that "the gifts and the call of God are irrevocable" (Rom. 11:29)—that is, God can be counted on to keep his word, to attain his goal. Were this not the case, God would have neither sovereignty nor freedom vis-à-vis human responses but be at their mercy. At the same time, Paul does not see God as a tyrant who forces his will on his subjects. After all, God's intent is human trust, not mere compliance. Paul's discussion moves in several steps.

First, he argues that the sovereign freedom of God means that God's dealing with Israel has never depended on human merit (or achievement), for that would make God's relation to Israel a matter of reward, compensation. Right from the start, God determined that Abraham's lineage would run through Isaac, not Ishmael (Rom. 9:6-8), because Isaac's birth was a matter of God keeping his promise. Subsequently, before Isaac's and Rebekkah's twins were born, Jacob was the chosen one. Clearly the choice did not depend on how the boys turned out, on their respective achievements.

Second, Paul raises objections (using the *diatribē* style): Is God unfair? No, because in Exod. 33:19 God says, "I will . . . show mercy on whom I will show mercy." Mercy, by definition, is not something that can be judged to be fair or unfair. Conversely, God's "hardening" Pharaoh's heart shows the same thing: God is free to achieve God's purpose as God wills

(Rom. 9:14–18). Now comes a double objection: If that is the case, why does God hold persons accountable for their actions ("Why does he still find fault?"), and, "Who can resist his will?" (i.e., Isn't God then a tyrant?). Paul declares these questions to be out of bounds because a creature cannot interrogate the Creator any more than a pot can ask the potter, "Why did you make me this way?" Paul then infers that God has put up with resistance from one group (the unbelieving Jews) in order to attain his purpose for others (the Gentiles and believing Jews; Rom. 9:19–24). Paul sees that through the gospel "then Gentiles who did not pursue righteousness attained . . . righteousness through faith" but Jews who did pursue righteousness by trying to obey the law failed to reach his righteousness because they rejected the gospel (Rom. 9:25–33, supported by quotations from Scripture). Romans 10, after restating Paul's gospel, ends with a series of quotations from Scripture which Paul believes interpret the present situation: "I [God] have been found by those who did not seek me" (the Gentiles) but God has extended his welcome continually "to a disobedient and contrary people." Still, God has not rejected Israel across the board, for Paul himself is proof to the contrary (11:1–2).

The fact that Paul and other Jewish Christians are a minority is nothing new, for already in Elijah's time there was but a remnant who did not succumb to Baalism. "So too at the present time there is a remnant, chosen by grace" (11:5). Structurally, the theological situation has not changed. In the process of achieving his ends, God has always had to cope with recalcitrant persons. Moreover, God's grace has never been anything but sheer grace, never a mere generous response to human achievement.

Third, Paul sees that through the Jews' rejection of the gospel, salvation has in fact come to Gentiles (Rom. 11:11). Paul is reflecting on a historical fact: when Romans was being written, the church was rapidly becoming predominantly gentile, and it may well have seemed to Paul that the rejection of the gospel by Jews and its acceptance by Gentiles were related in God's providence. As in Pharaoh's time, so now God uses the "hardening" of one to achieve his purpose with the other: "a hardening has come upon part of Israel until the full number of the Gentiles come in, and so all Israel will be saved" (Rom. 11:25–26). Paul never speculates on how this will happen. Had he done so he would have violated precisely the sovereign freedom of God, for knowing the "how" would imply that God could be manipulated, that the process could be hastened or slowed, that the achievement of God's intent was in human hands after all. (Paul's statement that he increases his ministry to Gentiles in order to make Jews jealous and so save some of them should not be taken as a strategy; see Rom. 11:13–14). But if Paul's trust in God is truly Abrahamic, then Paul must trust God to keep the promise with regard to all Israel just as Abraham trusted God to keep the promise with regard to the birth of Isaac.

Two things at least should be clear: (1) Although Romans 9—11 has been the main quarry from which stones for the Christian doctrine of predestination have been cut, nevertheless Paul's own agenda is quite different. He was not at all interested in explaining which individual would be saved and which not. He was reflecting on the mysterious ways in which things work out in history, on the fact that things turn into opposites (Israel should have said Yes but said No, while Gentiles said Yes; the No of the one produced the Yes of the other), and on the fact that neither the Yes nor the No is the last word. This is why in Rom. 11:17–21 he warns gentile Christians not to become proud. The sovereign freedom of God is just that—God's innate capacity to achieve his ends without coercion. (2) The deeper logic of Paul's discussion of Jews and Gentiles is identical with the logic underlying his discussion of justification by faith. Only a God who has sovereign freedom can make right the relation to the sinner, and do so on God's terms.

Newness and Constancy

The other polarity that makes clear how Paul understood the sovereign freedom of God is newness and constancy; specifically, the radical newness of the gospel and God's constancy. Can Paul affirm both? Or did his zeal for the gospel induce him to conclude that in Christ God had changed the rules? There is no doubt that Paul would have repudiated Marcion, as well as all forms of Marcionism still lurking in many Christian circles—that the OT God is one of law and wrath, but the God of the NT is one of gospel and grace. But then, how did Paul hold together the newness of the gospel and the constancy of God?

The theme of God's constancy surfaces as a problem of the law. If God's purpose has been a right relation to himself based on sheer trust, why did God give the law in the first place? In Galatians 3 Paul wrestles with this question.

Although certain details of the Galatian crisis continue to elude scholarly sleuths, the main point is clear enough: the gentile Galatian Christians were being persuaded that if they wanted to be first-class Christians they must accept circumcision. Thereby they would perfect their present, second-class status into which Paul's gospel had brought them. (The RSV obscures this by translating Gal. 3:3 as "Are you now ending with the flesh?"; the NEB is better: "Do you now look to the material to make you perfect?") The way Paul appeals to Abraham suggests that his opponents themselves had been appealing to Abraham, perhaps arguing that Abraham was circumcised *after* he was pronounced righteous by God—accordingly, circumcision follows faith as its perfecting sacrament. Apparently the Galatians did not understand that accepting circumcision implied accepting the obligation to observe the law, for Paul writes, "I testify again to every man who receives circumcision that he is bound to keep the whole law" (Gal. 5:2). Yet Christ has redeemed us from this obligation.

Then why did God give the law at all, especially after declaring Abraham to be righteous apart from the law? Did God change the rules? Does not what comes later supersede what preceded? Not at all, he argues, because a ratified will is not changeable (Gal. 3:15). That is, what God promised to Abraham's offspring cannot be claimed by anyone else. And who is Abraham's offspring? Christ! Moreover, those baptized into Christ are Abraham's offspring (v. 16, 29). In other words, the law given later to Moses "does not annul a covenant previously ratified by God" (v. 17). Were that the case, then God would change the rules of the game. But why then was the law given? "It was added because of transgressions" (RSV)—a phrase susceptible to differing interpretations. It probably means that the law was given either in order to restrain human sinning, or to deal with it (presumably through the sacrificial atonement system prescribed by the law), or perhaps both. In any case, Paul clearly denies that the law was given in order to make possible true life (as he understands it). Judaism's claim that obedience to the law, God's will in written form, leads to life reflects a misunderstanding of the law's capacity, "for if a law had been given which *could* make alive, then righteousness would indeed be by the law" (Gal. 3:4; see also Rom. 8:3). It is quite unlikely that "because of transgressions" means that God gave the law in order to *produce* transgressions, as Sanders claims (*Paul, the Law, and the Jewish People*, 66, 67, 144 ["attributed sin directly to the will of God"]). Sanders does see, however, that Paul says various things about the law's role, depending on the needs of the immediate argument, and that consequently it is virtually impossible to combine all the statements into a single, coherent "doctrine of the law." (In chap. 8 we will turn to the law in Romans; here we continue with Galatians.)

The function of the law (as something that deals with transgressions) is only temporary, for it was added "till the offspring should come to whom the promise had been made" (Gal. 3:19b)—that is, until Christ (and those in him). During that period (from Moses to Christ) "the law was our custodian" (better, our warden, or trustee who has charge for a time). But now that the Christ-event has occurred, "now that faith has come," we are no longer under the law. In Gal. 4:1–2 Paul paraphrases his point: a minor, though heir of the estate, "is under guardians and trustees until the date set by the father." But now that the preset time has come, the minor is no longer under the guardian but enjoys full rights of the son. And how do we know we are "sons"? Because the Holy Spirit in our hearts prompts us to call God "Abba!" (Papa). Through Christ God himself has terminated the time when the law was in charge, and God has confirmed this through the Spirit. If this be true, then the law is not opposed to God's promises categorically; the God of the gospel is not pitted against the God of the law, because it was God who "added" the law for a specific purpose and terminated its role at the set time.

Thus Paul argued that the way of the law was temporary and that its end was foreseen by God from the start. As he said in Gal. 3:8, Scripture preached the gospel to Abraham. Anyone who wants to be truly Abrahamic now lives by sheer trust in God, not by law. Thus God's sovereignty manifests itself not in God's freedom to change the rules arbitrarily but in the constancy with which God pursues and achieves what was promised to Abraham.

Paul no more asks, Why did God give a law which could not make alive? than he asks why the sovereign God permitted Adam to sin in the first place. Instead, he wrestles with the theological significance of what to him are undeniable facts: On the one hand, the New Age began with Christ, and now Gentiles who accept the gospel enjoy the same salvation as believing Jews, as the Galatians' own experience attests (Gal. 3:2–5). On the other hand, God promised Abraham that in him the Gentiles would be blessed (Gal. 3:8, citing Gen. 12:12; 18:18), and the law was given later to Israel. Since the gentile Galatians were being persuaded that circumcision is required, Paul's task is clear: So to coordinate these facts that it is obvious that accepting circumcision is nothing less than relapse from the new situation—comparable to engineers who, having begun to use computers, allow themselves to be persuaded that they must now begin to use slide rules. It is not surprising that, facing this situation, virtually everything

Paul says about the law in Galatians is negative. It is an interesting, though futile, exercise to speculate on what he might have said about the law had the Galatians rejected the law and all connection with Abraham. As it is, however, Paul connected all Christians with Abraham without relying on the law, and he did so by affirming God's constancy precisely in bringing to pass the new situation through Christ. What Paul could not do was to denigrate the law in such a way as to suggest that the law and the gospel are inherently contradictory (Gal. 3:21), for this would imply a self-contradiction in God. Paul's way of handling this problem is to coordinate them temporally, and to place them both under the sovereignty and constancy of God's purpose.

The newness of the gospel, then, does not reflect a U-turn in God's intent but a new time. Now the era of law is superseded because God's intent is being realized, inasmuch as Christ marks the time when God's promise is kept.

The theme of God's constancy in newness appears also in Romans. In Rom. 3:21–26 Paul characterizes the redemption in Christ, the *hilastērion*, as occurring to "show God's righteousness, because in his divine forbearance he had passed over former sins"; that is, God ratifies his previous forgiveness of sins. Paul appears to imply that precisely because the law could not give real life, a sacrificial system (epitomized by *hilastērion*) to mediate God's forgiveness was needed. That God had "passed over" sins before shows that God did not decide to be gracious on Good Friday. Hence Paul can assert that the gospel does not overturn the law but actually confirms what the law means (Rom. 3:28–31).

When Paul writes subsequently that "for everyone who believes Christ is the end of the law with respect to righteousness" (Rom. 10:4, au. trans.), "end" (*telos*) probably does not mean sheer termination (as Robert Badenas, *Christ the End of the Law,* has shown) but that with him the goal of the law has been reached and its role completed.

Creation and New Creation

Being rooted in Judaism and its Scripture, Paul assumed that God is the Creator. Rom. 4:17 refers to God as the one "who calls into existence the things that do not exist," as close to a statement of *creatio ex nihilo* as the NT contains. In Rom. 1:18–20 Paul appropriated the prevalent Hellenistic cosmological argument for the existence of God, namely, that the Creator can be inferred from the creation. But Paul transformed this motif by turning this commonplace idea into an indictment: first, by saying that what can be known of God is manifest because God has manifested it (rather than because human minds deduced it); second, this knowledge of God makes persons "without excuse." It does not secure their understanding of God.

Whereas the deutero-Pauline letters to the Colossians and Ephesians emphasize the relation of the pre-existent Son of God to creation (see chap. 3), the undisputed letters virtually ignore this. However, given Paul's appropriation of Jewish wisdom theology, and given the occasional nature of the letters as well, one should not infer that this theme was of no interest to Paul. As in the case of the Jesus-traditions, Paul might have said more in his teaching than he found germane to say in his letters.

What Paul does speak of repeatedly, however, is the host of malign invisible powers which now tyrannize creation. Again, the letters do not provide instruction about them, but assume that "everybody" knew what they were. The fluidity of Paul's terminology shows that he was not concerned to be precise at this point. In Rom. 8:38 he mentions angels, principalities (*archai*), and powers along with other threats to human life. In 1 Cor. 15:24 he writes of rule, authority, and power; Gal. 4:3, 9 has *stoicheia*, which RSV and NEB translate "elemental spirits of the universe." Doubtless Paul alludes to the same cluster of invisible powers that Eph. 1:21 calls rule, authority, power, and dominion, and that Eph. 3:10 calls "the principalities and powers in the heavenly places." Still, the undisputed letters do not say the same things about these powers as the deutero-Paulines: Paul himself does not say that the Christian fights "against the principalities, against the world rulers of this present darkness, against the spiritual hosts of wickedness in the heavenly places" (Eph. 6:12), nor that these powers, "whether thrones or dominions or principalities and authorities," were created through the pre-existent Christ (Col. 1:16), though he might have believed it. Paul never traces the human dilemma or the origin of sin to these powers; nor does he explain how they are related to "the god of this aeon" who blinds unbelievers to the truth of the gospel (2 Cor. 4:4); nor does he blame this "god" for the Jews' rejection of the gospel. Elusive as Paul's thought about these forces is, there is no doubt that he understood the human scene to be influenced by them.

More important to Paul was the view that there were two aeons: "this aeon and the aeon to come." Although Paul never uses the entire phrase, his references to "this aeon" show that he assumes the duality (Rom. 12:2; 1 Cor. 1:20; 2:6, 8; 3:18; 2 Cor. 4:4; "the present evil age" in Gal. 1:4

is a paraphrase). "Aeon" is not simply epoch; it is a way of characterizing the present world order as a whole. This way of speaking is rooted in Jewish apocalyptic which (a) saw all of history as a whole over against God's pledged redemption, yet (b) did not see any evolution or development from one to the other but regarded the new world order as God's radical alternative to the present. Apparently Paul believed that this change would occur in conjunction with the coming of Christ, the Parousia; but his letters show no interest at all in explaining that transformation. Though he says that "the form of this world (*kosmos* here = *aeōn*) is passing away" (1 Cor. 7:31), he never describes the age to come.

In Rom. 8:19–23 Paul writes about the redemption of creation from "futility" (NEB: frustration) and from "bondage to decay" (NEB: shackles of mortality)—evidently alluding to the "curse" that befell creation as a result of Adam's sin. Here Paul also says that creation waits eagerly "for the revealing of the sons of God," that is, for the full transformation of the Christian self, including the redemption of the body (see chap. 7). This will occur because "the creation itself will be set free from bondage to decay and obtain the glorious liberty of the children of God." This remarkable statement implies solidarity between persons and the created world, so that the redemption of the body—a piece of creation— carries with it the redemption of the whole creation. For Paul there is no such thing as a redemption that separates the self from the creation.

The importance of this theme for Paul was rediscovered by Ernst Käsemann who saw that for Paul God's act in Christ intends to reclaim and reconstitute creation. Seeing this element in Paul's theological horizon helps us understand what he meant by calling Christians "new creation" (2 Cor. 5:17; Gal. 6:15). For Paul the new life in Christ is a harbinger of the redemption of creation. Therefore whoever is in Christ is "new creation."

Participation and Anticipation

Participation and anticipation refer to two modes of thinking about salvation. This discussion of baptism and Lord's Supper (chap. 4) has already shown that for Paul the Christian participates in Christ. What needs to be done at this point is to reflect on the rationale of participation-language. Anticipation, on the other hand, is a basic Pauline way of thinking eschatologically about salvation. Grasping both modes of thought will make it easier to follow Paul as he clarifies certain theological issues (Part III).

Robert Tannehill identified what is important about participation: "Christ's death and resurrection are not merely events which produce benefits for the believer, but also are events in which the believer himself partakes" (*Dying and Rising with Christ*, 1). The Christ-event does not remain external to the believer. Nor does the gospel report only something decisive that occurred elsewhere (in Palestine) once upon a time (even if only two decades had elapsed when Paul reached Corinth). An event related externally to the self must be claimed by an act of will; the self repeatedly decides to make the past, distant event relevant by imitating it, by becoming a disciple of the figure. If the figure and his teachings are internalized, this process depends on the discipline and the disposition of the self. Moreover, internalizing an external event requires knowledge of the past, the Jesus-traditions. Finally, this normative tradition gauges whether the internalization is inadequate or inappropriate.

These somewhat abstract formulations actually describe Matthew's view of the relation between the believer and the Christ-event. For Matthew, the Christian is a disciple who is summoned to shape his or her life on the pattern of Jesus (Matt. 28:20). Making the Christian confession "Jesus is Lord" does not save, but doing God's will embodied in Jesus (Matt. 7:21–23). The most serious charge against the disciple, as against the Pharisees, is hypocrisy—the manifest gap between professing and performing. There is nothing in Matthew that corresponds to Paul's baptism into Christ, to participation in Christ, nor to Paul's emphasis on the Spirit who indwells the believer. Conversely, Paul's gospel did not call for a Matthean concern for a body of Jesus-traditions because Paul's believer was not a disciple of Jesus but a participant in the event. To contrast Matthew and Paul is not to declare one to be "better" than the other, but it is to see that they differ and that each has his own internal coherence.

Paul thinks holistically, in terms of the structures or wholes: Adam and Christ, Israel and Gentiles, law and grace, Spirit and flesh, etc. Each of these polarities is a structure of existence in which one participates, in which one's existence is defined because the participant is, by definition, "open" to and governed by the structure. The fact that these structures stand over against one another accounts for the either/or quality of much of Paul's thinking. Paul never understands the self to be autonomous, having the option of whether or not to participate in a structure. Paul's gospel therefore announces that emancipation from one structure is possible because participation in another is available.

The destructive contradiction that Paul points out, therefore, is not the Matthean one between confession and deed, but between conflicting participations. This is why Romans 6 points out that the person who has been baptized into Christ's death must regard himself/herself "dead to sin and alive to God in Christ Jesus" (v. 11); this being the case, one cannot live "in sin" and "in Christ" at the same time (v. 2). Of course Paul knew that Christians still commit sins, even if they are "freed from sin" (v. 7). But Paul is not talking about a sinless, perfect existence, as his exhortation shows: "Let not sin therefore reign" (v. 12). Rather he is talking about a transfer from one domain to another. Consequently the destructive contradiction consists of failure to actualize the transfer.

This thinking in terms of wholes, of structures of power in which one participates, can be seen also in the way Paul insists that whoever wants to be justified by the law has "fallen away from grace" (Gal. 5:4), for law and grace are modes of relationship which, because of the way each links one to God, are spheres of power in which one participates. As we shall see in chapter 7, this same participation-in-structures way of thinking also underlies Paul's statement in Rom. 8:7, "You are not in the flesh, you are in the Spirit." Everything depends on the kind of reality in which one participates.

One cannot simply decide not to participate in Adam, flesh, law, or sin because apart from a liberating event which incorporates the self into a new structure, such a decision would be a futile gesture. For Paul, however, the event of Jesus Christ is precisely such an alternative structure. To believe that, to be baptized into it, and to celebrate at the Table one's participation in it—these motifs are at the heart of Paul's gospel.

Anticipation is not an alternative to participation, but its eschatological horizon. This is because for Paul the Christ-event in which one participates is the eschatological event. Here lies the difference between Paul's participation theology and that of the mystery cults; in them, the participation is in an ever-repeated cycle and so is essentially timeless. Paul understood Christ as the eschatological event not because he knew Jesus had proclaimed the imminent coming of the kingdom, nor because he knew Jesus had understood that kingdom to be irrupting into human life through his mission, including exorcisms (Mark 3:20–27). Even if Paul knew these traditions he would have regarded Jesus as the eschatological event because of the resurrection.

We must bear in mind that Paul believed in resurrection as an eschatological event long before he became a Christian, for this was a basic tenet of Pharisaism, and of other types of Judaism influenced by apocalyptic. Although there was no standard scenario for the eschaton, resurrection was part of a sequence including judgment, rejuvenation of the world, and so forth. To believe that resurrection had occurred in the case of Jesus meant, therefore, that the End was beginning and that the new creation was at hand. The rest of the eschatological drama would surely follow without delay. Christ is thus the beginning of the New Age and those "in Christ" were participants in new creation.

Like other Christians of the time, Paul understood himself to be living between the "already" and the "not yet," somewhat the way participants in a new administration live between election day and inauguration day. Already those who participate in Christ live out of the impending future into the present. The future is no longer an extension of the present, but an alternative to it. To live by participation in what is not yet fully here is to live by anticipatory participation; it is to claim the life of the future ahead of time and so get out of step with the present. Participation accents the present accessibility of the future; anticipation accents the futurity of that in which one participates. Participation emphasizes the "already," anticipation the "not yet."

Paul's thinking is characterized by this dialectic between participation and anticipation. It marks not only his understanding of the sacraments, but also his ethics. Bultmann has shown that Paul's ethic is a dialectic of the indicative and the imperative—that is, the indicative states what one now is in Christ, and the imperative summons the believer to actualize what one is. Victor Paul Furnish (*Theology and Ethics in Paul,* 225) has insisted, properly, that the imperative "is not just the result of the indicative but fully integral to it." In other words, Paul's imperative is not grounded simply in what *is* ("Become what you are!") but in what *is underway*. The only way one can participate in an event still in motion is by acting with it.

PART III

WHAT PAUL FOUGHT FOR

Paul's theology was polemical because it was wrought in controversy. His letters struggle for the authentic meaning of the gospel. They never argue with persons or positions outside the Christian community, but with Christians within it. Non-Christians were addressed in Paul's preaching and in accompanying discussions (Acts 19:8-10). The more seriously the authentic meaning of the gospel was threatened, the more intense was Paul's response. Sometimes he wrote warmly (1 Thessalonians 1—3); at times magnanimously (as in Phil. 1:12-18); sometimes he was sarcastic (1 Cor. 4:8) or crude (Gal. 5:12). Paul's letters manifest his total engagement with the subject matter, his passionate commitment to the truth of the gospel.

The controversies provoked him to rethink fundamental themes and to clarify particular aspects of the gospel that he had preached and taught. In the following chapters we concentrate on three theological positions for which Paul fought. We shall first see how Paul contended for faith/trust as the wholly adequate way of salvation and mode of life (chap. 6); then how Paul inferred a radical Christian existence from the gift of the Spirit (chap. 7); and finally, how his view of God's righteousness uncovered dimensions of the human dilemma (chap. 8). These themes are not an outline of Paul's theology. The concern is not to tabulate and organize things Paul believed but to understand the major theological issues for which he contended.

CHAPTER SIX

DIMENSIONS OF TRUST

Repeatedly Paul had to defend and interpret his understanding of faith/ trust. Four major occasions elicited an especially concentrated effort. The first was at the Council of Jerusalem (Acts 15; Gal. 2:1-10); unfortunately for us, Paul's letters do not record how he made his case. The second was Paul's confrontation with Peter at Antioch (Gal. 2:11-14). The third place was Ephesus where Paul learned that Christians in Galatia were being persuaded to accept circumcision (see chap. 5) and that a similiar danger existed at Philippi, to which the letter fragment in Phil. 3:2-21 responds. The fourth occasion was writing the letter to Rome, although the exact purpose of writing precisely such a letter and sending it to Rome remains disputed.

Paul's theological understanding was not worked out in a vacuum but wrought in intense struggle with alternative views which also claimed to be Christian, indeed, more Christian than his. Krister Stendahl is right in what he affirms but wrong in what he denies. "Paul's doctrine of justification by faith has its theological context in his reflection on the relation of Jews and Gentiles, not within the problem of how *man* is to be saved. . . . The doctrine of justification originates in Paul's mind from his grappling with how to defend the place of the Gentiles. . . " (*Paul Among Jews and Gentiles,* 26, 27, italics his). Moreover, Paul's understanding of faith was indeed central, despite what Stendahl goes on to say. Rather, for precisely the reason Stendahl gave—Paul's call—his understanding of faith was the central issue because what legitimates Paul's vocation is precisely what is at the center. Nor may Stendahl's statement be taken to mean that Paul's theology is not concerned with "how *man* is to be saved," for Stendahl writes of the *context* and of the *catalyst* of Paul's theology (where the doctrine of justification "originates"); he does not speak of the *content.* We shall see that Paul's thought was indeed concerned with how man (*der*

Mensch, not *der Mann*) is saved, precisely because this is what his view of Jew and Gentile before God implied.

Our discussion will be guided by three questions: First, is trust/faith really adequate, or must it be supplemented? Second, if salvation by trust/faith means freedom from the law, from obligation, is Paul consistent in making moral demands on his readers? That is, does the emphasis on sheer trust dissolve the necessity of doing, or conversely, does the continuing need to do (and not do) certain things compromise the competence of trust to rectify our relation to God? Third, does Paul's emphasis on faith alone not lead to "conservative ethics"?

The Adequacy of Trust/Faith

The earliest literary defense of the adequacy of trust/faith was also the most vigorous, namely, in the Letter to the Galatians. In Gal. 2:21 Paul concludes his comments on his previous confrontation with Peter by saying, "If righteousness [right relation to God] comes by law, then Christ died for nothing" (NEB), a reformulation of 2:16. Why does not law—living according to law—produce a right relation to God? Paul gives various answers to this question, depending on the immediate context and occasion. Because the Galatians were persuaded ("bewitched" is Paul's word, 3:1) to make their life perfect by means of circumcision, Paul first argued that this contradicts their own experience of the Spirit (3:1-5).

That the Galatians had entrusted themselves to God as presented in the gospel, had been baptized and so received the Spirit (see chap. 4), was not in question. In question was whether that was good enough, whether circumcision could enhance what they already received. It is difficult for us to understand why anyone could have thought so, for today non-Jews commonly have their newborn males circumcised, and the rationale for doing so has nothing to do with religion. In antiquity, however, one explanation which Hellenized Jews gave for the operation was that cutting off a bit of skin manifested disdain for the fleshly self and signaled commitment to controlling the power of the flesh. The call to circumcision was credible to the Galatians on some such basis—that this operation ratified and enhanced their commitment to the Spirit and its struggle against flesh (understood as the "lower nature," not as Paul understood it; see chap. 7). So Paul asks, How did you get the Spirit in the first place? By obeying commandments or by believing the gospel? (Gal. 3:2). If the latter, then the

Spirit has nothing to do with "the works of the law." Law and Spirit represent different structures of reality (see chap. 5), and are mutually exclusive ways of dealing with flesh.

In other words, Paul spread the gospel and founded churches on the assumption that trust/faith, followed by baptism and the receipt of the Spirit, was the response that was both wholly appropriate and fully adequate for salvation and participation in the body of Christ. In the Galatian crisis, however, he saw a threat so subtle and so powerful that if he did not turn the situation around his entire mission would have been pointless (Gal. 4:11). Either righteousness—the right relation to God and all that this entailed, including participation in Christ and receiving the Spirit—comes through trust/faith or it does not: "If righteousness were through the law, then Christ died to no purpose" (Gal. 2:21), because on that basis the gentile Galatians could have become righteous by becoming law-observant proselytes to Judaism long before Paul preached the gospel or "faith came" (Gal. 3:23, 25).

This odd expression, "faith came," shows that Paul understands trust/faith as a fundamentally new possibility, as nothing less than a mode of existence—grounded in a way of relating to God—not available before or without the gospel, and hence not available before or without Christ (which accounts for the juxtaposition of similar phrases in Gal. 3:23–25— before faith came, until faith should be revealed, until Christ came, now that faith has come). Because Paul sees trust/faith as a new mode of existence made possible by Christ and the irruption of the New Age into the present, he regards also its alternative as a mode of existence, as a way of life, including a way of relating to God. From this angle, it does not finally matter whether that alternative is polytheism or Judaism, for neither is defined by the New Age in Christ. Later, Paul will actually write, "Are we Jews any better off? No, not at all; . . . all, both Jews and Gentiles, are under sin," as well as, "there is no distinction, since all have sinned and fall short of the glory of God" (Rom. 3:9, 22–23).

This perspective requires us to see how Paul can tacitly equate being under the law of Moses and being under the *stoicheia*, as he does in Gal. 4:1-11. Evidently, for reasons not stated—the Galatian readers knew them—the Galatians not only were acceding to the demand for circumcision but were resuming the veneration of astral powers, observing "days and months, and seasons, and years" (Gal. 4:11)—practices probably associated with astrology, thereby acknowledging that the *stoicheia* still controlled human affairs, even of Christians. Whether circumcision was somehow interpreted in relation to these forces is not known. In any case, for Paul what the Galatians were doing all amounts to the same thing— relapse into the domain of law. In order to establish the adequacy of trust/faith, Paul had to expose the Galatian alternative by showing what was really at stake.

One thing is clear at the outset: Paul's construal of the situation, and of the law, differs fundamentally from that of the unnamed teachers of the Galatians as well as from Judaism's own understanding of the law because he views it from the standpoint of the new situation, "now that faith has come." For Paul, "faith" here is a kind of shorthand for the whole Christian dispensation, which the issue at hand focuses on being redeemed from bondage, freed, whether from the special, temporally limited guardianship of the law in the case of the Jews, or from the generic enslavement of Gentiles to the *stoicheia*. The Jew, like a child placed for a time in the custody of a guardian, is "no better than a slave" so long as he/she is a minor (Gal. 4:1–2). So too the Galatians were "slaves to the elemental spirits of the universe" [RSV for *stoicheia;* Gal. 4:1–3], "in bondage to beings that by nature are no gods" (v. 8). This construal of the Jewish and gentile situation prior to and apart from the trust/faith response to the gospel makes it extremely improbable that E. P. Sanders is right in claiming that "Paul's criticism of Judaism, rightly understood, does correspond to Judaism as revealed in its own literature"—i.e., to its own self-understanding (*Paul, the Law, and the Jewish People,* 63 n. 142).

Since the "empirical" difference between Jews and Gentiles was doubtless clearer to Paul, the ex-Pharisee, than to most of us, it is evident that his understanding of the law proceeds from a different starting point, and has in view a different content as well. What allows Paul to put life under the law and life under the *stoicheia* under the same rubric—bondage? Since he does not explain, we must attempt to infer his reasoning. Paul sees that common to both is that the individual finds himself/herself in a web of obligations with divine sanctions, obligations which must be met if one is to be rightly related to God/the gods. In this context, the real meaning of law, *nomos,* for Paul is not provided by the Jewish view of Torah (which also means instruction, guidance). Rather, Paul's eye is on the impingement of the law on the self, and this leads him to discern the "lawness of law," whatever the particular law might be. In other words, in his own way, Paul thought phenomenologically about law. Because Sanders denies this (*Paul, the Law, and the Jewish People,* 158), he cannot make Paul's reasoning intelligible (e.g., "few parts of his letter are more illogical than those in which he equates the status of Jew and Gentile prior to faith," 151), but must be content with thinking that by formulating the problem correctly ("the plight of Jew and Gentile must be the same, since Christ saves all on the same basis," 69) he has at the same time accounted for it.

If human existence under law is bondage to a divinely sanctioned structure of obligation which must be met in order to be rightly related to God, be it law epitomized by circumcision or by *stoicheia,* then one can understand why Paul's theological analysis of law shows no interest whatever in distinguishing one law from another: for example, the ritual from the moral, the permanently valid from the transient, the fair from the unfair, for the problem is not certain laws but law. If one bases life on law, if one's relation to the divine is the result of meeting requirements, it does not really matter under which law one's life takes shape.

Paul came to such a radical conclusion partly because of his missionary experience. If the gentile Galatians, by trust/faith alone, could be rightly related to God and receive the Spirit—the same salvation that Christianized Jews like Paul, Barnabas, or Peter enjoyed—then clearly nothing constitutive of their Jewishness is a precondition for receiving the full benefits of Christ. In this light, for Gentiles to allow themselves to accept circumcision as a requirement for becoming bona fide Christians is nothing other than being "severed from Christ" and falling away from grace (Gal. 5:4).

The fact that it was the Galatian crisis that elicited from Paul such a vehement defense of the adequacy of faith led Sanders to claim that "righteousness by faith . . . serves primarily as a negative argument against keeping the law as sufficient or necessary for salvation," and that "the real bite of his theology lies in the participatory categories," not in the juridical ones which deal with the law and justification (*Paul and Palestinian Judaism,* 492), though he recognizes that Paul links them (502) and that finally they amount to the same thing (506, 508). Even this concession is finally unsatisfactory, however, because Paul's argument is inherently negative and positive at the same time. A resolute affirmation of the adequacy of trust/faith to relate one rightly to God will always appear "negative" with respect to every other mode that, however subtly, supplements sheer reliance on what God has done in Christ with prerequisites.

Theologically, the demand for "circumcision" can take many forms, even today. It appears whenever one thinks along these lines: "Faith in

Christ is fine as far as it goes, but your relation to God is not really right and your salvation not adequate unless . . . " It does not matter how the sentence is completed. Whenever such fine print is introduced to qualify trust/faith, there is "circumcision," and Paul's defense of the adequacy of trust/faith can come into its own again. The Galatian situation is never far; in fact, it is all too familiar.

Faith's Freedom and the Obligation to Love

Paul's polemic against the "works of the law" as a prerequisite to the right relation to God can generate the impression that, on the one hand, Paul dissolved moral obligation altogether (thereby misreading "You are not under law but under grace"; Rom. 6:14), and on the other hand, that he was inconsistent by also insisting that Christians live according to certain norms. Moreover, Paul can even use the phrase "the law of Christ" (Gal. 6:2; 1 Cor. 9:21). If we do not grant that Paul was fundamentally inconsistent, as I do not, then we must see how faith's freedom from the law and moral obligation cohere in Paul's thought. In other words, our theme concerns the relation of Pauline faith and Pauline ethics. We will first reflect on Paul's overall stance, then look at a specific instance.

Several aspects of Paul's stance are important. First, we have seen that for Paul there is no autonomous self, a person wholly free from sovereignty and its obverse, obligation. To be a person is to be in a sphere of influence, to have one's existence shaped by a controlling factor outside the self. Paul implies that obligation is built into humanness, for obligation is the correlate of sovereignty. Accordingly, trust/faith does not abrogate obligation categorically, nor emancipate one from obligatory norms absolutely. Rather, trust/faith in God, and the attendant life in Christ and in the Spirit, transfers the self to another domain, where Christ is the norm because he is the Lord. This transferal from one domain to another, both of which entail obligation, underlies the whole argument in Romans 6. Being emancipated from the domain of sin means being "enslaved" to God and to a new righteousness. Obligation is now defined by this new situation, and by its Lord. In other words, Paul's ethics is intimately linked with Christology and soteriology.

Second, when Paul wrote of "the law of Christ" he did not simply substitute Christ for Moses. That would be only a cosmetic change in the human situation. Sanders rightly points out that the righteousness in Christ is different because it is in Christ and so depends on trust/faith (*Paul and Palestinian Judaism*, 551). Philippians 3:10 clearly contrasts two kinds of rectitude: "my own, based on law" and "that which is through faith in Christ, the righteousness from God that depends on faith." Were this not the case, being baptized into Christ would be only a changing of the guard and the old way of becoming right before God would still be in effect. Under law, meeting God-given obligation was a way of attaining a right relation to God. But for whoever is rightly related to God by trust/faith, obligation is not a means to an end but the daily actualization of the end already reached by anticipation. Precisely because it is reached by trust which leans into the future for its vindication on judgment day, the right relation to God is not a manifest goodness to which one could point, but something that must be made actual constantly. Hence Paul exhorted the Philippians, "work out your own salvation with fear and trembling; for God is at work in you" (Phil. 2:12–13). "Work out" does not mean "devise," but make effective, make actual.

The ethical meaning of the already/not yet is the dialectic of the indicative and the imperative: You are in Christ, live in Christ. Herman Ridderbos (*Paul,* 254) correctly says that the relation of the indicative to the imperative must not be reversed. One does not strive to live by the Spirit in order to be in the Spirit. Indeed, the shift from being in the domain of law to being in the domain of grace reverses the relation of the indicative to the imperative. As Paul sees it, in the domain of law, the imperative is supposed to lead to the indicative (but does not; Rom. 7:10), but in the domain of grace where trust/faith prevails, the indicative generates the imperative.

Contemporary ethicists have repeatedly argued whether an "ought" can be derived from anything other than an "is," the given, say, biological makeup. An externally derived obligation is probably unattainable—like requiring a turtle to fly. But for Paul, the "is" (the indicative) is an "is" of eschatological existence imparted by the Spirit to those who believe. Therefore the "ought" which arises from this "is" is discontinuous from obligations arising from an empirical "is," at least in certain aspects. Because there is new creation, the ethic of Christian existence appears so strange and discontinuous from the ethic of this world (see 1 Cor. 4:11–13; 2 Cor. 11:30). In other words, Paul's obligatory norm is not grounded in the potentiality of this age but in that of the age to come, in which the believer participates by trust/faith. Yet it is shaped by the tension between this age and the next.

Third, because Paul is not a proto-Marcionite, the will of God for the age to come cannot be pitted against the will of God as made known in this age. Accordingly, Paul appropriates certain fundamental moral mandates accepted in the current world, and never indicts the content of the law but rather insists that it is holy, just, and good (Rom. 7:12). What was right in the law of Moses cannot be contrary to what life in Christ should produce. Rather, the Christ-event occurred "in order that the just requirement of the law might be fulfilled in us, who walk not according to the flesh but according to the Spirit" (Rom. 8:4). Elsewhere Paul identifies this core of the law as the command to love the neighbor (Rom. 13:8–10; Gal. 5:14). Since also Judaism regarded this command as the summation of the law, we must ask, "How did becoming a Christian change this point?" It changed the domain in which the love-command is heard. According to Rom. 8:4, the right obligation is fulfilled by those who have the Spirit. According to Gal. 5:22 love is the fruit of the Spirit, and according to 1 Corinthians 13 it is the chief gift of the Spirit. Paul does not mean that the Spirit simply helps the Christian do what the law requires, as if one were still in the old aeon. Were that the case, then the relation of the self to law's obligation to love would not have been changed at all; only the self's capacity would have been enhanced. But the game plan would be the same. Rather, the Spirit is the power of the New Age, present in the midst of the old; it is power for moral action in the domain of the new creation, of which it is the pledge. Therefore "the just requirement of the law" is to be fulfilled by those whose life in the Spirit anticipates new creation. Unless this is clear, one understands the Spirit as a booster in one's capacity to do the will of God under the aegis of the Old Age in which one seeks to establish a right relation to God by achievement.

Paul's understanding of faith does not dissolve obligation, nor does his understanding of obligation undermine his contention that faith is adequate to relate one rightly to the righteous God. When the Epistle of James polemicizes against a separation of faith from works, and contends that one "is justified by works and not by faith alone" because "faith apart from works is dead" (James 2:14–26), it is not Paul that is hit by this salvo but a vulgarized "Paul" who has been distorted into implying that faith is assent to doctrines. Paul's sense of moral obligation is not one iota weaker than that of James. For Paul, Christian obligation is grounded in the Christ-event and in the impingement of the new creation on the present age whose time is running out. For James, however, obligation is not grounded christologically at all. Therefore obligation in Paul is actually stronger.

We turn now to a specific instance in which Christian freedom from the domain of law manifests itself in the obligation to love within the new creation. Paul's understanding of Christian freedom must be distinguished from all views that regard freedom as absence of restraint so that the self can be fulfilled, and that see the limits of freedom where self-actualization impinges on the freedom of another. According to a popular view, one is free when one can do as one wishes, so long as one does not harm another. In Paul's understanding of freedom, however, the self is always in a sphere of power in which one has a Lord and a brother and sister. For Paul, therefore, the brother or sister does not limit freedom but provides the occasion to make it concrete.

We see this in Paul's treatment of an issue that appears at first glance to be rather remote and trival—dietary matters, especially those having to do with meat "offered to idols." In antiquity there was a connection between sacrifice and slaughter. Animals sacrificed in the temples were not totally burned or given to the priests; often the meat was sold to the public after part of it was used as sacrifice. It may have been rather difficult to buy meat that had not been associated with the temple. When the Corinthian Christians discovered that this situation posed some problems, they asked Paul about them in their letter to him. He responded in 1 Corinthians 8. In 1 Corinthians 10 he deals with a closely related matter, eating sacred meals in the temple precincts. The relation between these chapters is unclear (see chap. 2). In Romans 14—15 Paul also deals with matters of diet, but there the problem is not "idol meat" but vegetarianism. Here we concentrate on 1 Corinthians 8.

Modern translations put some phrases into quotation marks because it seems clear that Paul is quoting slogans being used in Corinth, perhaps even in the letter sent to Paul. What were the Corinthians saying? (*a*) "All of us possess knowledge." (*b*) "An idol has no real existence" because "there is no God but one"—a reference to the Shema. (*c*) According to 1 Cor. 10:23, another slogan was "everything is permitted"—there are no limits on freedom. (This slogan appears also in 1 Cor. 6:12, which we shall discuss in the next chapter.) These slogans suggest that the Corinthians took seriously Paul's teaching of freedom from the law and of monotheism; there could be no danger in eating meat that had been offered to nonexistent gods. But some Corinthians did not have this knowledge (1 Cor. 8:7)— apparently they had it in their minds but not in their emotions and sensibilities. They could not eat this meat in good conscience; the associations with the shrines were simply too strong. Moreover, socioeconomic differences might have been an additional factor, if Gerd Theissen is correct. ("The Strong and the Weak in Corinth: A Sociological Analysis of a Theological Quarrel," in *The Social Setting of Pauline Christianity,* 121–43).

How did he respond? (*a*) Paul did not argue with the slogans, nor with the theology of those who claimed freedom to eat anything they chose. He agreed with them. Here we see how far Paul had come from Pharisaism. In v. 8 he says, "Food will not commend us to God. We are not worse off if we do not eat, no better off if we do." (*b*) Paul did not regard the scrupulous as obstacles to be overcome but as an occasion to make Christian freedom concrete. Instead of urging the scrupulous to "get with it," he urges the free to be radically free—to be free from asserting their freedom if this means ruining a person whose conscience is "weak" (1 Cor. 8:9–13). How is the "weak" Christian destroyed by the "strong" who freely eats anything, anywhere? The reasoning is not explained here, but appears in Rom. 14:23: the weak person may be induced to "go along," to eat meat without being fully persuaded that this is permissible. Then the weak person does not act out of knowledge or the freedom of living by sheer trust in God, but out of fear of being embarrassed. Then the person who eats actually does sin, because "whatever does not proceed from faith is sin." Thereby the free person's exercise of freedom occasions sin by "ruining" a fellow Christian's relation to God. Although Paul is convinced that the free person is right, he says that if his own attitude toward food causes another Christian to violate conscience, he will become a vegetarian (1 Cor. 8:13).

The scruples of fellow Christians are not an obstacle to the exercise of freedom but the opportunity for it, because not until one is free also to forgo the exercise of one's freedom for the sake of a fellow-Christian is one really free. True freedom is not a matter of everyone seeking his or her own good ("doing one's thing" unless it infringes upon another) but a matter of seeking the well-being of another. Love is more than doing good as an act of charity; it is an act for the well-being of the brother's or sister's relation to conscience and to God.

In 1 Cor. 10:1–22 the problem appears to be somewhat different, namely, whether Christians can participate in the Lord's Supper and in sacred meals at shrines as well. Here Paul forbids double participation because he believes that pagan sacrifice is actually given to demons. In 1 Cor. 10:25–33, however, the concern is with private meals, and Paul says flatly, "Eat whatever is sold in the meat market without raising any questions on the ground of conscience." Here Paul tries to move the weak toward the position of the strong. If invited to the home of a non-Christian for a meal, one is to eat whatever is served without raising questions of conscience (v. 27). But if someone else points out that the meat had been offered to idols, one is not to eat it—again in order to respect the conscience of the person who pointed this out (vv. 28–29), presumably a fellow Christian.

Paul's overall position is clear. He himself agrees with the free and the strong. Anything may be eaten. But because not all Christians are as strong as this in faith, he will *exercise* his freedom by *not insisting* on his freedom, so that the brother's and sister's relation to God may be a matter of faith— even if it is still weak faith.

A "Conservative" Ethic?

Paul's ethics sometimes disturbs people on several fronts. (*a*) Paul's ethics is pastoral throughout, oriented to and motivated by his concern to "build up" the Christian community. Paul is not concerned with the actions of non-Christians (1 Cor. 5:12). He is interested chiefly in the impression they get of the Christian group (1 Thess. 4:11–12; also 1 Cor. 14:23–25). Although he does not limit "doing good" to Christians alone (Gal. 6:10), he does not summon the church to community service, to participate in community life as responsible citizens, to be a "servant people." Still, Paul's theology and ethics open the door for Christian involvement in society, but Paul himself did not walk through it. It would have been ludicrous if he had urged small house churches to pretend that they had civic responsibility. (*b*) E. P. Sanders charges that Paul's theology of righteousness by faith "does not lead to ethics" (*Paul and Palestinian Judaism,* 492), evidently because Paul did not make the connection explicit. One may well ask, however, whether Sanders's conclusion is not premature. (*c*) Paul's ethics appears to be so thoroughly influenced by his expectation of the imminent Parousia that it produces a "conservative" stance, for he actually urges his readers not to change their roles in society (1 Cor. 7:17–24, 29–31). It is this passage, and the issues generated by it, that concern us here.

The passage begins with Paul's rule in all his churches: "Let everyone lead the life which the Lord has assigned to him, and in which God has called him" (v. 17). Then he applies this to three situations: circumcision (vv. 18–20), slavery (vv. 21–24), and marriage (vv. 25–40). In the first two instances he concludes with an imperative, "let him/her stay put" but in the third case he merely states a preference—it is better to stay unmarried

(vv. 26, 40). Paul's general reasons for insisting that both the circumcised and the uncircumcised stay as they are have become clear already; the point is: neither circumcision nor uncircumcision "counts for anything" (Gal. 6:15).

His word to the Christian slave is of the same order, though stated differently. The slave who becomes a Christian is the Lord's freedman though he/she still belongs to an earthly master. Similarly, the free person who becomes a Christian is Christ's slave. How to translate v. 21 is problematic. The RSV has, "If you can gain your freedom, avail yourself of the opportunity," but S. Scott Bartchy's dissertation (*Mallon Chrēsai: First-century Slavery and the Interpretation of 1 Corinthians 7:21*) demonstrates that the NEB's alternative rendering is probably to be preferred (and more distressing to moderns): "Even if a chance of liberty should come, choose rather to make good use of your servitude." If this is the meaning, then Paul relativized slavery and freedom. Attempts to change one's status tacitly make that status more important than it ought to be for one whose relation to God is a matter of trust/faith. What matters is not socioeconomic freedom but inner freedom in Christ.

Inner freedom that is not tied to external status in society was a common theme also among Stoics. They held that because every person bears the logos, reason, or a spark of the divine, each person can be equally free inwardly, where it counts, in order to live rationally, whether one is a king or a slave. Real freedom consists in mastering that over which one has irradicable control—the decision to live rationally and wisely. No one can confer that freedom or take it away; it is an inalienable capacity (analogous to our "inalienable right"). One can, of course, forfeit it. Nothing therefore is to be taken so seriously as to restrict the self's capacity to live by reason; especially are matters of custom, institutions, bodily needs and desires, and business interests to be regarded with suspicion because they insinuate their claims on the inwardly free self and reduce it to bondage. So the Stoics urged an inner distancing from the world and a deliberate indifference to it.

What Paul says to the slave appears to echo Stoic understanding of inner freedom. Similarly, his counsel to unmarried Christians expressly emphasizes the importance of being free from anxieties (v. 32). He urges "those who have wives to live as though they had none, and those who mourn as though they were not mourning, and those who rejoice as though they were not rejoicing, and those who buy as though they had no goods, and those who deal with the world as though they had no dealings with it" (vv. 29b–31). What separates Paul from the Stoics here is the eschatological horizon, manifest at the beginning and at the end of this passage (vv. 29a, 31b). In other words, the Stoic inner distancing is grounded in the nature of the self; Paul's is grounded in the eschatological hour—"the form of this world is passing away." Because this world and its institutions, structures, social status, and so forth, have no future, Paul urges that Christians not involve themselves in it more than they must, and to make no effort to change their socioeconomic status in it. To put Paul's counsel colloquially, "Don't hustle to join or change a lame-duck administration."

Many readers today have difficulty with (*a*) Paul's assumption that because inner freedom is what matters, attempts to change one's situation make the externals more important than they really are; and with (*b*) Paul's concern for distancing oneself from the world. Resistance to both points stems from the same base—the conviction that people's inward state is in fact conditioned by their external situations. On the other hand, one should not overlook the fact that a measure of inner freedom is always available even to the oppressed, the prisoner, and the poor, and when claimed manifests itself as a certain pride and dignity.

Other readers today suspect that Paul was not as faithful to his own insights as he should have been. According to 1 Cor. 12:13, all Christians were "baptized into one body—Jews or Greeks, slaves or free." According to an apparently pre-Pauline baptismal formulation in Gal. 3:27–28, for Christians "there is neither Jew nor Greek, there is neither slave nor free, there is neither male nor female." To be in Christ is to participate in new creation in which these socioeconomic distinctions have lost their significance. (See Elisabeth Schüssler Fiorenza, *In Memory of Her,* chap. 6.) Why, then, did Paul not insist that one should translate this eschatological reality into present social reality? Did he refuse to draw the consequences of his own theology? Or did he overreact against those who did?

It is often inferred that the Corinthians were enthusiasts because, among other things, they did translate Paul's theology into a social program among themselves. If so, then Paul opposed them because he was convinced that until the Parousia one could not live only by the "already." The new creation was accessible only by faith, not by achieving changes in social relationships. Paul denied that one was already, unambiguously, manifestly saved to the extent that one could abrogate the structures of the present world. Paul's seemingly "conservative" stance may well have been his attempt to guard against the illusions of "over-realized eschatology" which was claiming too much for the "already."

Interestingly, Paul assumed that some change was appropriate and necessary. Both his insistence that circumcision was really irrelevant, and hence merely a matter of custom, and his indifference to food laws show that he was in fact creating a new style of community. Moreover, in his churches women exercised leadership; the whole discussion of women wearing veils while prophesying (1 Cor. 11:2–16) assumes that they speak in church as well as the men. Unfortunately this same discussion shows that in what Paul regards as a matter of "proper" conduct, he was not as free as he could have been or should have been.

Paul's successors who wrote in his name were more conservative than he was. They not only forbade women to participate in the church services (1 Tim. 2:11–12), but also appealed to lists of household duties (*Haustafeln*) which circulated in popular moral discourse. In these lists of duties, not in Paul's own letters, we find admonitions that wives must be subject to their husbands (Eph. 5:22; Col. 3:18; Titus 2:3–5), and husbands to wives. In these materials slaves are urged to be obedient but masters considerate (Eph. 6:5–8; Col. 3:22—4:1; 1 Tim. 6:1–2). Indeed, Titus 2:9–10 is concerned about the behavior of slaves toward their masters but does not say a word about the master's treatment of the slaves. Paul was far less conservative than what was written in his name.

In the last analysis, what makes Paul appear "conservative" socially is our loss of his eschatological horizon. Once the sense of the imminent end is gone, Paul comes through as a social conservative who urges that everyone stay in his or her place regardless of how long history and society continue. Appealing to 1 Corinthians 7 to say that Paul argues against all social change actually stands the apostle on his head. Paul does not sanctify the status quo as a divinely ordained order but insists on precisely the opposite—it is doomed to pass away. It is not society's inherent goodness or rightness that causes Paul to urge Christians not to change their relation to social structures or the social structures themselves, but the conviction that God will soon change everything anyway. Actually, then, by depriving the status quo of its divine sanction, of its inherent rightness and permanence, Paul opened the way for Christians to change the world once they ceased to rely on God's impending act to do so. Paul's ethics is really not conservative at all, but lays the foundation for an ethic of social involvement. He himself built very little on this foundation. Yet here too, one might recall Paul's own words in 1 Cor. 3:10:

> According to the commission of God given to me . . . I laid a foundation and another . . . is building upon it. Let each . . . take care *how* he builds upon it.

CHAPTER SEVEN

SPIRIT AND BODY

Paul's view of Spirit and body is more easily, and more commonly, misunderstood than anything else he wrote, and the consequences are serious and extensive. Paul himself sensed it. In fact, his correspondence with Corinth is dominated by the fallout of their misunderstanding and his attempts to correct it. Romans 8 is also important, for it mentions "Spirit" more often than any other chapter in the NT.

Our discussion will clarify the source of common misunderstanding, namely, Paul's contrast between Spirit and flesh; then we will note Paul's view of body-salvation. Finally, we shall see how Paul's understanding of Spirit, body, and flesh affects his ethics. But before engaging Paul's letters, three general observations are appropriate.

First, we reflect on what a theological discussion of the divine Spirit involves. Christology is a theological understanding of the Jesus-event. Although classical Christology includes both the pre-existence and the post-existence of Christ, the core has remained focused on Jesus, a public figure who can be investigated according to accepted canons of historiography. Pneumatology, the doctrine of the Spirit (from *pneuma,* wind or spirit), on the other hand, is a theological understanding of what is not a public but an intensely personal experience which no one sees. At most, one can see a certain behavior, such as speaking in tongues or healing, which is regarded as a manifestation of the Spirit, but neither the Spirit nor the experience of it is an observable public datum. Not even the person having the experience can observe it. Pneumatology deals with the most intimate, and sometimes intense, experience of the divine. Moreover, although for purposes of discussion one can distinguish human from divine Spirit, one cannot actually isolate one from the other in order to be sure that one is talking about only one and not the other. Consequently, the more one emphasizes the working of the divine Spirit, the more one emphasizes also one's collaboration with it. Paul appears to be the first Christian theologian who recognized this.

Second, it is difficult to appreciate the role of the Spirit in early Christianity because our own attitudes intrude. Those who, for whatever reason, are gun-shy of the Holy Spirit, charismatics, or "spiritual healing" may have difficulty appreciating the early Christian experience. The "charismatics" and their sympathizers may find that the early Christian experience differed considerably from what they prize. For example, one can as easily imagine Paul announcing a Spirit-healing service as one can imagine him throwing a Halloween party.

Numerous aspects of the early Christian experience of the Spirit have been noted already and need not be repeated. Only three things should be mentioned here: (1) In the NT no one receives the gift of the Spirit privately. (2) The divine Spirit was power, a divine power divinely given, not simply heightened human power. This is why it was called the *Holy* Spirit. (3) This gift of divine empowerment was understood as a hallmark of the New Age, and therefore given to every believer by definition. At the same time, some persons apparently had received an extra measure of the Spirit—the prophets, such as Agabus (Acts 11:27–28) and Philip's four unmarried daughters (Acts 21:9).

Third, Paul too can be regarded as a prophet or as a charismatic figure, although he never designated himself this way. In any case, he had visions and ecstatic experiences (1 Cor. 9:1; 14:18; 2 Cor. 12:1–4), worked miracles in the Spirit (2 Cor. 12:12), and even disciplined a wayward Corinthian *in absentia* (1 Cor. 5:3–4). What Paul fought for was not the legitimacy of the experience of the Spirit but the proper understanding of it.

Spirit and Flesh

It was in Corinth that the issues became most acute. The Corinthians were drifting toward what would later become full-blown, aggressive Christianized Gnosticism. They appear to have interpreted the Spirit in a gnosticizing way, that is, in terms of traditional Greek metaphysical dualism which Gnosticism intensified. The gnostic believed that he or she *is* a spark of the divine Spirit to begin with, and that this divine essence has been trapped in a physical, mortal body. The body caused the divine self to forget its nature and so forfeit its destiny. The later gnostic myths will explain how this entrapment occurred. There is no evidence that such myths were circulating in the Corinthian church in Paul's day, nor that the

Corinthians were using the slogan *sōma-sēma*—the body *(sōma)* is a *(sēma)* tomb. But their thinking apparently was moving in that direction. Accordingly, salvation was construed as release from matter, body, history. Nothing interested a gnostic more than one's "soul's salvation." (Frequently, gnostics blurred the distinction between the soul and the spirit.) If the spirit or soul were not redeemed it would be entombed in one body after another. Salvation comes to this entrapped self when it learns who it really is, where it came from, what its real plight now is, and what its destiny will be when the present body dies—the self will soar homeward to be reunited with its divine counterpart.

Apparently, the Corinthians understood the experience of the Spirit as a confirmation of this self-understanding. One should bear in mind that "ecstasy" means standing outside oneself, and that "enthusiasm" means having God within. These are simply alternate ways of verbalizing the same event: the divine enters the self, or one's spirit leaves the body to make contact with the divine. That is, as divine spirits the Corinthians either escaped the body during moments of ecstasy or were contacted by invading divine power in times of heightened enthusiasm. Speaking unintelligible language (the "language of angels") was a sign that one's spirit had momentarily escaped the stifling influence of the mortal body. Those who manifested these experiences were deemed to be the most "spiritual." The wandering preachers who undermined Paul's influence after he departed apparently traded on this mentality.

Since Paul shared some of the same views and experiences, his problem was how to clarify and correct the misunderstandings in Corinth without denying or denigrating the experience of the Spirit itself. First Corinthians 2—3 shows how far Paul can go in affirming a "charismatic" understanding of Christian teaching and experience. But Paul immediately turns the affirmation into an indictment of the readers: "I could not address you as spiritual persons [*pneumatikoi*, pneumatics] but as fleshly persons" [*sarkikoi*, from *sarx*, flesh]. Paul did not accuse them of being "fleshly" because he denied that they had experienced the Spirit, but because they misconstrued its meaning. The factions that had emerged (1 Cor. 1:11–12; 3:3–4) showed Paul that they were "fleshly" because cliques emerge when people champion one leader over another because one is more impressive than the other. Doing this means relying on criteria that any observer would use. But to assess the gifts of the divine Spirit by the criteria of human culture is a self-contradiction. Such spirituality is most fleshly pre-

cisely in trying to be spiritual in the wrong way. This passage shows that
Paul uses "Spirit" and "flesh" in ways that might surprise today's readers
no less than his original ones.

What does "Spirit" mean in Paul's thought? To begin with, Paul shares
the early Christian understanding of Spirit as eschatological gift of power;
the divine presence is a gift received, not an essence released (Rom. 8:15;
1 Cor. 2:12; Gal. 3:2).

Also, he regarded the Spirit as a sign that the New Age is already dawn-
ing, and receiving it is a mark of one's participation in the future. The two
metaphors that express this understanding appear to be uniquely Paul's:
down-payment (*arrabōn;* 2 Cor. 1:22; 5:5) and first-fruits (*aparchē;* Rom.
8:23). The *arrabōn* is not so much a guarantee (as the RSV renders it) as
a pledge (as the NEB has); the word used to be rendered "earnest" as in
"earnest money" in real estate. Earnest money is paid to indicate that the
buyer will complete the transaction without delay. The *aparchē* language
comes from the OT law that required the first of the harvest to be given
to God as a token of the whole crop which is about to be ripe. In Paul's
mouth, both metaphors express the conviction that the Spirit means inauguration, not consummation. Both celebrate the present gift as something
that points ahead, as a reality that characterizes Christian life between the
"already" and the "not yet."

Because Paul never defends these metaphors, it is clear that the Corinthians did not dispute this understanding of the Spirit. They too affirmed
it, because also they regarded the experience of the Spirit as anticipation
of salvation. But for them, this salvation was release from the body. In
other words, what divided Paul and the Corinthians was not the idea that
the Spirit is a pledge of the future but the sort of future that is pledged.

Ernst Käsemann has emphasized repeatedly that Paul did not separate the
gift from the Giver. That is, God remains sovereign, indeed, exercises sovereignty in giving this gift, and does not become a dispenser of power that
operates independently. Thus Spirit is field of force, a power structure in
which the recipient operates as a subject in a kingdom. Romans 8:9 makes
it clear that being "in the Spirit" as a domain of power and having the
Spirit "dwell in you" are simply alternate expressions.

The letter the Corinthians had sent to Paul asked about spiritual gifts;
Paul responded in 1 Corinthians 12—14. Although the word that introduces
the response in 12:1, *pneumatikoi,* can be either masculine or neuter, the
context indicates the latter is meant—"spiritual things." The most difficult

part of these chapters is 1 Cor. 12:1-3, where Paul insists that "no one speaking by the Spirit of God ever says, 'Jesus be cursed!' " Did the Corinthians actually curse Jesus when they were under the influence of the Spirit in their assemblies? Walter Schmithals affirmed that they did—they cursed the born, earthly Jesus because they were committed to the heavenly, spiritual Christ (*Gnosticism in Corinth,* 124-30). This interpretation has found little assent; the passage remains obscure.

The rest of the discussion deals with the gifts of the Spirit, *charismata* (from *charis,* grace; the gifts are "begracements"). Paul insists that the diversity of gifts is for the common good of the community. There should be neither boasting nor sense of inferiority. So Paul compares the community with a body. Christians with less impressive gifts should no more feel left out than a foot should feel inferior because it is not a hand. Conversely, Christians with more impressive gifts who disdain the others are as foolish as the eye who says to the hand, "I have no need of you." Just as many diverse organs make up a body, so the church has diverse persons with diverse gifts (1 Cor. 12:4-31); the Spirit actually enhances individuality.

In this context, Paul shares the "ode to love" because he regards love as the chief gift of the Spirit which all can have (1 Corinthians 13). Whereas the prized gifts of prophecy, tongue speaking, and knowledge *(gnosis)* are transient, love endures, along with faith and hope.

In 1 Corinthians 14 we read about the problematic and divisive gifts in Corinth—speaking in tongues and prophesying. Tongue speaking (glossolalia) is unintelligible speech; prophecy is intelligible. Paul does not want to stifle either one, but to put them in proper perspective. He prefers prophecy to tongue speaking because intelligible speech benefits the whole congregation, whereas glossolalia benefits only the individual—unless someone "translates" the sounds into something that makes sense (1 Cor. 14:1-5). Consequently, if there is no interpreter present, the tongue speaker should keep silent and speak only with himself and God (1 Cor. 14:28). Paul's counsel not only subordinates the most striking gift of the Spirit to the needs of the community, but also implies that the tongue speaker *can* hold his or her tongue (at least control the volume), that one is not simply "carried away" and has no responsibility for what happens. The same is true of prophets. Verse 32 denies that the power of the Spirit puts one into a mantic state in which all self-control is lost: "The spirits of the prophets are subject to the prophets." (Interestingly, according to Gal. 5:22 self-control is one of the gifts of the Spirit!)

Paul is also concerned lest the ardor for the gifts of the Spirit destroy the order of the church's assemblies. If everyone tongue-speaks at once (as they apparently did), a guest will conclude that this group has gone mad (1 Cor. 14:20–23). On the other hand, because prophecy is intelligible, orderly prophesying might induce a guest to conclude that "God is really among you" (v. 25). Paul's overriding concern is that "all things be done for edification" (v. 27)—not pious sentiment ("edifying thoughts"), but for the development of the community. Paul also urges that the congregation evaluate what the prophets say and not accept everything just because a person speaks under the influence of the Spirit (1 Cor. 14:29).

Near the end of his discussion, Paul makes a little "dig" at the Corinthian enthusiasts: anyone who thinks he is a prophet or a Spirit-person should recognize that what Paul says is the Lord's command—because Paul too is a person in the Spirit. One Spirit-insight should acknowledge another. Whoever disagrees with Paul, therefore, is not as "spiritual" as he or she claims to be. One suspects that here Paul's sense of apostolic office overrides everything else; otherwise Paul too would have to accede to what the Corinthians might say in the Spirit.

Throughout his letters, Paul says almost nothing about the nature of the Spirit, its relation to God or Christ (2 Cor. 3:17 is an exception). The benediction in 2 Cor. 13:14 simply juxtaposes Father, Son, and Spirit. Strictly speaking, then, Paul's letters do not teach a pneumatology. Paul's concern is rather the theological and ethical meaning of having received the Spirit.

Having seen how Paul interprets the experience of the Spirit, we now turn to its opposite—flesh (*sarx*). First, for Paul, *sarx* is not identical with *sōma,* body, nor is it the substance of the body. Rather, like Spirit, flesh is a domain of power, a sphere of influence in which one lives. Failure to see this is the core of the misunderstanding mentioned at the beginning of this chapter.

Here Greek thinking can easily mislead us. Greek thought was not uniform by any means. Nonetheless, one strand of it was interested in the essence of things, something almost wholly absent from Hebraic thinking. Consequently, Greek thought concerned itself with the nature of the soul (or spirit) and its relation to mind and body. The metaphysical dualism the gnostics emphasized was ancient already in Plato's time (fifth century B.C.), but received its decisive shape in his hands. In this tradition, the body retards the capacity of the soul or spirit because their essences are incompatible. The lingering effect of Greek thought manifests itself in the unfortunate translation of Romans 8, where NEB translates "flesh" as "lower nature." This is precisely what Paul does *not* mean. Wherever flesh is understood this way, one misconstrues Paul's dualism of flesh and Spirit as a struggle between the divine Spirit and our bodies, the locus of "our lower nature."

Paul's understanding of flesh is rooted in the OT, where flesh is not a constituent element of the self, a "lower nature" at odds with a "higher nature," but a way of characterizing the whole self vis-à-vis the divine. Thus when Isa. 40:5 promises that "all flesh" will see the revealed glory of God, it refers to all humanity; when Isa. 40:6 says, "All flesh is grass" which withers in comparison with the word of the Lord, it is the transient nature of human life as such that is in view, not "lower natures." Likewise, Isa. 31:3 says, "The Egyptians are men and not God; their horses are flesh and not spirit" because "flesh" means creatureliness, transitoriness. A human, like a horse, is flesh because neither is divine. "Flesh" is not a neutral term used to describe dispassionately a "nature" or an "essence"; it is an evaluative term which signals the weakness, transitoriness, unreliability of phenomenal existence.

Second, Paul also uses "flesh" when we expect him to use *sōma,* body. For instance, "weakness of the flesh" in Gal. 4:13 means susceptibility to illness; 2 Cor. 12:7 speaks of Paul's "thorn in the flesh" (nobody knows exactly what this was); 1 Cor. 7:38 mentions "afflictions in the flesh" (RSV: "worldly troubles"), and in Phil. 1:23 "remain in the flesh" means "stay alive." Rom. 2:28 contrasts true circumcision with that which is "manifest in the flesh" (RSV: "external and physical"). Likewise, Gal. 2:20 refers to "the life I now live in the flesh." Yet even when Paul uses *sarx* this way, the term has a connotation which is devaluative, not simply neutral. There is a pathos to his use of "flesh" because it hints at primarily the creaturely, contingent, vulnerable, transient character of life. This is also clear in passages where Paul speaks of "flesh and blood" (Gal. 1:16; 1 Cor. 15:30). In all these passages, "flesh" interprets the empirical in light of the transcendent. Just as "this age" is always a valuing term in light of "the age to come," so "flesh" characterizes the empirical in light of Spirit.

Third, we need to see that Paul did not so much interpret the Spirit in light of flesh but the reverse; his understanding of the Spirit illumined what flesh really is. It is highly unlikely that Paul's understanding of flesh was part of his pre-Christian theology, even if the OT is its formal origin.

Rather, like everything else in Paul, the starting point was Christ and the Christian experience of God's grace. E. P. Sanders is right on target when he insists that "Paul's thought did not run from plight to solution, but rather from solution to plight" (*Paul and Palestinian Judaism*, 443). This is as true of "flesh" as it is of "law."

Paul's understanding of flesh appears in some of his characteristic expressions. (*a*) A major phrase is "according to the flesh." In Rom. 8:4, walking (= living) according to the flesh is contrasted with walking according to the Spirit (so also v. 5). The contrast is implied even when only "according to the flesh" is mentioned, as in 2 Cor. 1:17 (where RSV and NEB have "like a worldly man") and 2 Cor. 5:16 (RSV: "from a human point of view"; NEB: "worldly standards"). To live "according to the flesh" is to have the norms and values of life determined by the merely phenomenal, the frail and transient instead of by the Spirit which is transcendent. (*b*) The same is true of the adjective "fleshly" (*sarkikos* or *sarkinos*), as in 1 Cor. 3:3. (*c*) Romans 8:6 contrasts the "mind set" of the flesh with that of the Spirit. (*d*) "In the flesh" is the counterpart to being "in the Spirit" as Rom. 8:9 clearly says: "You are not in the flesh, you are in the Spirit." It is the Spirit as a sphere of power which has suggested that its opposite, flesh, is also a sphere of power.

Fourth, even though Paul can pit flesh and Spirit against each other (as in Gal. 5:17 or Rom. 8:7–8), he does not equate flesh and sin. The only passage that might suggest that he did is Rom. 8:3, for here he interprets the incarnation as follows: "God . . . sending his own Son in the likeness of sinful flesh . . . condemned sin in the flesh" (RSV). The phrase "sinful flesh" renders "of flesh of sin" and appears to characterize flesh itself as sinful. Yet "condemned sin in the flesh" distinguishes flesh from sin, so that it appears that the two are linked closely but not actually equated. This is why sin was condemned in its stronghold. (One should not overinterpret "in the likeness of" here, as if Paul implied that Christ assumed flesh that only looked like ours but was really different because his flesh was sinless; this introduces precisely the equation of sin and flesh that is not characteristic of Paul.) Flesh is a domain of power in which sin operates. That is why sin is condemned there. The center of the human predicament is not flesh but sin, living according to, setting the mind on, flesh.

In short, because Spirit is the power-sphere of the new age, flesh is the power-sphere of the old age. The struggle between Spirit and flesh is not a battle between higher and lower nature, between our bodily drives and our minds or spirits. Rather, the struggle is between the power of the eschatological future and the power of the empirical present.

In this light, we can now turn to Paul's understanding of body (*sōma*). For Paul, the central meaning of "body" is the actual self, what we might call the psychosomatic entity that I am. If "flesh" is a devaluing term, "body" is much more neutral. Paul never uses the phrase "according to the body." Frequently one can translate it "self." For instance, the RSV renders Rom. 12:1 literally as "Present your bodies as a living sacrifice" but the NEB correctly renders *sōma* here as "your very selves." This use of "body" appears in our term "somebody" and in the lines of the song, "When a body meets a body coming through the rye." Because Paul does not share the Greek view of the self as a spark of divine essence, he would not say "I have a body" but "I am body." Yet he does speak of "my body" (1 Cor. 9:27), hinting that one's actual existence is an object of one's action and will, that one can distinguish oneself from oneself, as Rudolf Bultmann puts it (*Theology of the New Testament,* 1:195–96). Because *sōma* refers to the actual self and not merely to one's physical body, we need to see how Paul relates salvation to *sōma*.

Body with a Future

For Paul salvation is for the body, the actual self I am. Here Paul's difference from gnostic anthropology manifests itself, for Paul does not believe salvation is a release of the soul *from* the body but a redemption *of* the body (Rom. 8:23). The presence of the Spirit is a pledge of this, as Rom. 8:11 makes explicit: "If the Spirit of him who raised Jesus . . . dwells in you, he . . . will give life to your mortal bodies also through the Spirit which dwells in you." According to Phil. 3:20, it is Christ "who will change our lowly body to be like his glorious body," not extract an eternal soul from it.

The fullest exposition of Paul's understanding of body-salvation begins by reminding the readers that they had accepted the gospel centered in the death and resurrection of Christ (1 Cor. 15:1–11). But now some are saying, "There is no resurrection of the dead." Had they changed their minds? There is no reason to conclude that they denied the resurrection of Christ; in fact, Paul points out that what they deny contradicts what they have believed about Christ (vv. 13–19). It is likely that they denied resurrection categorically (not life after death). If so, then they probably interpreted Christ's resurrection as the release of his eternal soul or spirit from the body. In any case, for them "There is no resurrection of the dead" was not a word of despair but a triumphant assertion of the victory of spirit over matter. Like Paul, the Corinthians believed that what was true of Christ is true of themselves also. They also agreed fully with Paul, "Flesh and blood cannot inherit the kingdom of God" (v. 50). From these two agreements, however, they were drawing opposite conclusions.

Paul points out that Christ has been raised from the dead, not released from a mortal body, and that his resurrection is the first fruits of resurrection (v. 20), the prototype. What happened to Christ will happen to "those who belong to Christ" (v. 23). That is, Paul uses the agreed-on principle "as Christ, so we" against the Corinthian denial of resurrection.

In answering the questions, "How are the dead raised?" and "With what kind of body do they come?" Paul makes it clear that he understands resurrection to be transformation, not resuscitation. (This is true of the NT as a whole.) The heart of Paul's contention is, "We shall all be changed" (vv. 51–52). To illustrate his point, he appeals to the transformation a kernel of grain undergoes when it "dies": it is buried a brown seed but comes up a green plant—the same, yet different. To undergird his analogy, he points out that "not all flesh is alike" (a rare neutral use of "flesh"), in order to argue that there are also different bodies, earthly and heavenly ones (vv. 35–41). Although the rationale is not altogether cogent, what Paul is driving at is stated in v. 44: "If there is a physical body, there is also a spiritual body." So the mortal body is planted in the ground, but it is raised "in glory"; it is planted "a physical body, it is raised up a spiritual body." Nowhere else does Paul mention this "spiritual body" and it is hard to know just what he had in mind. What is clear, however, is that a totally disembodied existence is repudiated.

In 1 Cor. 15:25–28 Paul had identified the final enemy to be overcome as death. In vv. 53–54, however, Paul subtly introduces another way of talking: "the corruptible" and "the mortal." Death the enemy is not the same as mortality, for the former is a usurping tyrant over human life, whereas the latter is a qualification built into the body ("flesh and blood cannot inherit . . . "). By shifting to this terminology, Paul tacitly grants that the gnosticising perception of the human problem cannot be dismissed out of hand; if salvation is for the body-self then the inherent mortality must be dealt with. Defeating an external tyrant, death, does not yet deal with this inbuilt defect. But instead of following the Corinthian solution, Paul argues for an alternative: transformation of the mortal body. It "puts on" immortality—that is what "we shall all be changed" means. In other words, even if the human situation is understood in Greek terms, Paul solves it in Jewish-Christian apocalyptic terms, for the transformation will occur at the Parousia. Thus he can cite Isa. 25:8 and Hos. 13:14, here understood as proclamations of eschatological triumph over death.

In 2 Cor. 5:1–5 Paul also discusses this eschatological transformation, but now contrasts the two modes of existence as an earthly tent and an eternal, heavenly house. The passage is somewhat obscure, but the core of the matter is clear: although Christians "groan and long to put on our heavenly dwelling," they do not desire to be "unclothed"—deprived of body categorically. Rather, the longing is to be "further clothed" so that what is mortal may become immortal. Here too the Spirit is the pledge of this transformation.

Paul shows no interest in describing the resurrection body, nor does he hint at where the new mode of existence will be lived. In 1 Thess. 4:13–17 he simply says, "The dead in Christ will rise first; then we who are alive . . . shall be caught up together with them in the clouds to meet the Lord in the air; and so we shall always be with the Lord." What interests Paul is the "thatness" of resurrection as transformation of actual human existence. In Phil. 1:21–23 he appears not even to have room for resurrection, for he speaks of being with the Lord immediately after death. How all this hangs together is not clear. He might not have been as logically consistent as we would like him to have been. It may also be that he simply called attention to certain aspects of the future hope that he deemed relevant to the argument at hand, and assumed the rest. "The rest," of course, is what we very much want to know.

What is at stake theologically is the understanding of God the Creator and of the self. Views of post-mortem existence which are based on the release of an eternal essence from a temporal, mortal body imply that the body is unredeemable, and hence they tacitly indict the Creator for making such a thing in the first place. They also imply that the divine essence is eternal, that it too pre-exists but somehow comes into a body. In other words, such views easily lead to the idea of the transmigration of eternal souls from one body to another. Difficult as Paul's view may be, it at least avoids these consequences.

Body Ethics

The ethical significance of Paul's theology of body manifests itself throughout his letters, but we shall consider only a few passages from 1

Corinthians and Romans. In 1 Cor. 6:12–20 we meet the basic theological position: "The body is not meant for immortality, but for the Lord, and the Lord for the body." Paul provides several warrants for this. (1) "God raised the Lord and will also raise us up by his power. Do you not know that your bodies are members of Christ?" Paul's rationale seems to be the following: (*a*) Christ's resurrection transformed him (as *sōma*/self). (*b*) His resurrection is the prototype of resurrection to come, of Christian somatic selves. (*c*) Christ's present Lordship lays a claim on the body/self, destined for resurrection. (2) Because body equals self, Paul can express this claim by saying that the *sōma* of the Christian is an organ ("member") in the body of Christ. (3) "Your body is a temple of the Holy Spirit within you." The mortal body/self is not a prison for the Spirit but its shrine. The body/self does not inhibit the Spirit; the Spirit, being stronger, sanctifies the body/self. Sanctification is not an intense religious experience but a moral process which hallows the self. (4) "You are not your own; you were bought with a price"—a metaphor derived from the slave market. Redemption means belonging to Christ, whose death was the (implied) price paid. So the moral meaning of having the Spirit is the imperative: "Glorify God in your body"—the actual selves you are. Paul's ethics is body-ethics.

All this was said over against the Corinthian trend, which spawned two opposing ethics. On the one hand, if one believed that the gospel brought to light one's essence as Spirit, and if one regarded baptism in a hyper-sacramental way, then one could develop a freewheeling ethic. One could proclaim, "I am free to do anything." If the Lordship of Christ has to do with the eternal Spirit in the self, then it does not matter what one does with one's body. Indeed, one might even make a point of demonstrating freedom by deliberately violating customs, taboos, and laws that control activities of the body. On the other hand, if one believed that the physical body was inherently hostile to the Spirit, then one might develop an ascetic ethic designed to thwart the body and its drives. The Corinthians pursued both strategies; inevitably, matters of sex and marriage brought the issues to a head.

The former style probably explains the case of the man who married his stepmother, contrary to both Jewish and Roman law (1 Cor. 5:1–2). Evidently she was not a Christian, for Paul says nothing to *her*, in accord with 1 Cor. 5:12. Beyond excluding *him* from the group, it is not clear exactly what disciplinary action Paul called for (vv. 3–5). More important, some Corinthians evidently were proud of him for he dared to live out his theology. His action is not the consequence of Corinth being "that kind of place," but a deliberate strategy designed to manifest his self-understanding.

The latter style led other Corinthians to write Paul about sex and marriage. Paul's response is in 1 Corinthians 7. It is not clear whether the opening statement in 7:1 is a slogan in Corinth (as the alternate translation in the NEB has it) or whether it is Paul's own view: "It is well for a man not to touch a woman." Either way, he agrees with it as a general principle— but then he ignores it as he deals with the problems at hand. Instead of explicating the metaphysical or moral rationale of this principle and then applying the result to the questions asked, Paul proceeds in an eminently practical, down-to-earth manner. In other words, Paul affirms sexual continence as a "good" but regards it as a special gift of the Spirit (one of the *charismata*), not something that applies to everyone (1 Cor. 7:7-8). O. Larry Yarbrough's dissertation discusses Paul's marriage counsel in light of ancient views of marriage (*Not Like the Gentiles: Marriage Rules in the Letters of Paul*). A concise treatment of Paul's views of sex, marriage, divorce, and homosexuality is found in Victor Paul Furnish, *The Moral Teaching of Paul.*

Paul's views of sex and marriage, when gauged by modern sensibilities, are often disdained. Yet in his context, they are much less male-dominated than similar treatments by Cynic-Stoic contemporaries or parts of the Jewish Wisdom tradition.

The Jerusalem Bible brings out the point of 1 Cor. 7:2 by explaining, "Since sex is always a danger . . ." (The New Jerusalem Bible omits this addition to Paul's text.) Nowhere in the entire discussion is there any positive assessment of sex as a means of enhancing mutuality or of expressing love and tenderness. But such a view of sexuality is a modern one, and we must no more expect to find it in Paul than we should expect him to advocate dental hygiene. In light of the Corinthian options, however, his views are rather "advanced." Paul does recognize that sex is a powerful drive, and he refuses to claim that having the Spirit neutralizes its power. So he tells the Corinthians that, given the dynamics of sex, everyone should be married (v. 2), unless one has the special Spirit-gift capacity to remain single. That singleness may be chosen for other reasons perhaps never crossed his mind.

Paul then discusses sex within marriage (1 Cor. 7:3-6). The point is that husband and wife belong to one another; neither is to regard the other as an object for self-gratification. Neither is to deny the other the "right" to sex. Moreover, if one of them should insist on refraining from sexual activity for the sake of religious devotion (like giving it up for Lent), this must be by mutual consent, and for a limited time only. Not only does Paul insist on parity within marriage in a way that was considerably ahead of his time, but he tacitly says, "Don't think you are so 'spiritual' that you can forgo (or be denied) sex indefinitely without serious consequences. You are not *that* saved." In other words, Paul's advice to couples is designed to disabuse them of their illusions about sex and the Spirit. He refuses to allow religious devotion to become the pretext for withholding sex from one's spouse.

In 1 Cor. 7:8–9 Paul counsels the unmarried and widows to remain single, but if their sexual drives create frustrations, they should marry "for it is better to marry than to burn" (with frustrated passions). This strikes moderns as a rather low, utilitarian view of marriage; the current mode of dealing with the situation—cohabitation without marriage—is not even discussed, for it never entered Paul's mind as a viable option. Paul's view of marriage is not a romantic one, to be sure, but again it must be seen for its impact in Corinth. Paul offers not a word of solace to those who, in the name of the Spirit, take it upon themselves to deny fulfillment of sexual drives. Precisely the opposite. He urges people to avoid frustration, not by hyperspirituality, but by getting married! The highly problematic passage in vv. 36–38 makes the same point with reference, apparently, to the engaged: "Let them marry—it is no sin."

The parity that Paul advocated for the Christian man and wife he extended also to households where only one of them is Christian (1 Cor. 7:12–16). If either non-Christian spouse is willing to stay married, the Christian should not seek divorce. Clearly Paul does not want the gospel to break up households; his attitude is quite different from that of Matt. 10:34–37. Moreover, Paul believes that the sanctity of the Christian spouse is imparted to the non-Christian spouse; otherwise, "your children would be unclean, but as it is they are holy" (1 Cor. 7:14). Unfortunately Paul's rationale is not stated as clearly as it might have been, but the main point is manifest: the Christian is not defiled by having sex with a non-Christian spouse; one does not have to protect the Spirit. Nonetheless, if the non-Christian spouse wants a divorce, one is not to contest it. Paul makes it clear that this is his word, not the Lord's (v. 12).

He makes it equally clear that it is not he but the Lord who commands that Christians not divorce each other (v. 10), but then adds a revealing phrase, "but if she does . . . " (and implies "but if he does . . . "). Paul is aware that in the changed circumstances of Corinth, he cannot insist on literal compliance with the word of Jesus, and that "mixed marriage" is something Jesus never had to face.

In 1 Corinthians 7 Paul's body-ethic expresses itself in his concern to give constructive counsel designed to enhance marriage and family life. Not a word appears about the evils of the body or of sexuality; not a line encourages the Corinthians' asceticism for metaphysical reasons. There is not a hint that the Spirit might be diminished by normal family life or that it makes family life impossible. In vv. 32–35 he does point out that concerns for domestic life might well distract from concern for "affairs of the Lord" just as he says that this world has but little time left (vv. 29–31). But these are practical considerations, not metaphysical ones. Paul's body-ethic is not negative, even though he clearly rejects certain behavior without ado (1 Cor. 5:11; 6:9–10).

Finally, Paul's body-ethic calls for a new attitude toward suffering. According to Rom. 8:18–25, having the Spirit does not immunize one against the world's suffering but actually enlivens the awareness of participating in it. Paul alludes to Genesis 3, according to which God "cursed" the ground, along with Adam and Eve: creation was "subjected to futility" and now exists in "bondage to decay." Yet because Paul thinks telically (in terms of *telos,* the end), he insists that God's action was not the last word, for this subjection is to be terminated, evidently at the Parousia when creation will be liberated and transformed. In the meantime, creation groans, yearns for redemption. Paul says all this to set up v. 23: those who have the Spirit also groan, like creation, as they wait for the future redemption of the body/self. Because the body/self is part of creation, the more intense the experience of the Spirit, the more awareness of the yet unredeemed character of existence, all of it. Paul implies that just as Christ's resurrection is the first fruits of the redemption of body/selves, so the existence of Spirit-bearing selves is the first-fruits of the redemption of all creation. The presence of the Spirit is an assurance of God's commitment, and so Christians need have no fear of suffering for it cannot separate them from God (Rom. 8:31–39). How could it, when God's own Son suffered as part of the God-given mission to redeem creation? In this light, Paul can say that "we rejoice in our sufferings"—not because we enjoy them but because the Spirit has been given so that now suffering can yield a positive moral meaning (Rom. 5:1–5). Suffering is no longer an index of how one stands with God (Job's problem). Rather, how one stands with God is an index of how one may regard suffering.

CHAPTER EIGHT

THE MORAL INTEGRITY OF GOD AND THE HUMAN SITUATION

Believing in God is not enough. Everything depends on the God in whom one believes and to whom one entrusts his or her life. Paul saw this clearly.

The Christ-event, centered in Jesus' cross and resurrection, revealed God decisively and thereby uncovered the character of the human situation as well. The cross/resurrection was the hub to which all spokes of Paul's theology were joined; procedurally, the cross/resurrection was the starting point for Paul's theological thinking. Paul did not, and could not, fit the Christ-event into the understanding of God that he inherited. Rather, his encounter with Christ compelled him to rethink everything from the ground up (which is not to say that he repudiated his heritage). As E. P. Sanders noted in *Paul and Palestinian Judaism,* Paul did not work out his theology as a solution to a set of problems with which he had been wrestling unsuccessfully. Rather, it was in light of the universal salvation wrought by cross/resurrection that Paul discerned the real character of the human problem.

Christian apologists commonly begin by first analyzing the human situation in categories which the non-Christian, it is hoped, will acknowlege; then they present the Christian faith as an answer. We do not know whether Paul used this strategy in his preaching, as Acts 17 in fact has him do (unsuccessfully!). His letters, however, show his thought moving in the opposite direction—from solution to plight. The title of this chapter reflects that movement of thought.

We shall first probe Paul's understanding of God as the rectifier of the ungodly. Then we shall see how Paul's insight into the character of God illumined the human situation. Finally, we shall note how the character of God affected Paul's attitude toward the future. Inevitably, many aspects of these themes have been touched before. It is appropriate, however, to pull some of the threads together in a discussion of the heart of Paul's theology for which he contended.

The Rectifier of the Ungodly

One of the most radical understandings of God in the NT cannot be found in a concordance because the term "God" is not used—namely, the one "who justifies the ungodly" (Rom. 4:5). This statement is of a piece with other characterizations of God in Romans 4: (*a*) the one "who gives life to the dead and calls into existence the things that do not exist" (v. 17); (*b*) the one who "raised from the dead Jesus our Lord" (v. 24). Like Rom. 5:8, these formulations express Paul's keen awareness that the cross and resurrection reveal the disparity between God and the prevalent understandings of God. The Christ-event disclosed the God one can really count on because it made clear God's commitments and his capacity to keep them, God's moral integrity.

The adjective "moral" should not be taken to mean that God is "moral." Rather it simply distinguishes what is in view here from ontic integrity— the oneness and unity of God's being. The unity of God's being is not something Paul discussed or defended in his letters. They show no awareness that statements about Christ as the Son of God or the Wisdom of God in any way compromised monotheism. What Paul did contend for is the constancy, consistency, dependability, trustworthiness, faithfulness of God in light of Jesus' cross and resurrection. It is these aspects of the integrity of God which the term "moral" indicates in the phrase "the moral integrity of God." When is God's Godhood most characteristically and significantly manifest? When God is decisively self-consistent, what happens to the world? To reflect on such themes is to reflect on the moral integrity of God.

"The moral integrity of God" is not Paul's phrase, of course; it restates the point of a phrase which he did use—the righteousness of God. To grasp Paul's radical understanding of God therefore requires us to attend to rather technical philological matters, though only the most salient will be noted here.

We begin with the semantic problem created by the limitations of the English language. "Righteousness" and "justice" are used to translate the same Greek noun Paul used, *dikaiosynē;* similarly, "righteous" and "just" render the same adjective *dikaios*. When we translate the verb *dikaioō*, however, we use the Latin "justify" since we cannot say "rightify." But righteousness and justice do not mean exactly the same things, and certainly "justify" commonly does not mean "to make right" but to provide reasons for, even excuses ("He is justifying himself again."). Given the divergence between justice and righteousness in common parlance, it is inevitable that most people make no connection between righteousness and justification. But in Paul's usage, they are simply different semantic forms of the same idea. When Kendrick Grobel translated Rudolf Bultmann's *New Testament Theology,* he proposed using the old English term "rightwise" for "justify"; however, "rectify" is less archaic and will be used here. In other words, to justify is to rectify, make right—not just (fair, equitable).

Although Paul wrote Greek, his meanings are derived from the OT and its understanding of right, righteous, and so forth. (*a*) The Hebrew term *ts-d-q,* and its various forms, refers to a relationship, to a norm, not to an inherent quality that we might call "righteous" or good. Righteousness is rightness. The specific meaning of righteous/righteousness depends on the norm in view. For example, in Genesis 38, the widow Tamar dressed like a whore in order to seduce her father-in-law Judah because according to Hebrew law he should have arranged for her to marry the deceased's brother in order to have children (for reasons of social and economic security in that society). Deprived of her "rights" she managed to become pregnant with Judah. When confronted by this situation, Judah said, "She is more righteous than I"—not meaning that she is morally better but that she was more in right relation to the norm than he had been. To be *ts-d-q* is to keep faith with what is right, with what is the right thing to do for the persons involved.

(*b*) In this light, we can understand Judges 5:11, which speaks of God's military victories over the Canaanites as his "righteousnesses" (note the plural!)—events in which God did what was right by Israel in light of his covenant commitments. Similarly, when Isa. 51:5 puts in parallel lines (indicating virtual equivalent meaning) "my *ts-d-q*" and "my salvation," it is clear that righteousness means God's deliverance (RSV) which accords with what is right for God to bring about. Such deliverance manifests God's integrity in keeping commitments.

(*c*) A verbal form of the Hebrew means "to make right," to rectify a relationship; in judicial matters it means "declare to be in the right" (as in "on the right side of the law"). It does not mean "make righteous" in the sense of making "good." If one is falsely accused and acquitted, one is "justified"—declared to be in the right after all, vindicated, as in Isa. 43:26, where God urges, "Set forth your case, that you may be proved right" (justified). Amos had a vision of a leaning wall (Amos 7:7-9), doomed to fall because it was not plumb (upright). Had his vision included an alignment to the plumb line, he could have said that the wall was "justified"—made right (not made a good wall). The same usage underlies Jesus' comment about the publican in the temple who confessed his sins, "this man went down to his house justified"—his relation to God had been made right. In such cases "to justify" means to correct, to rectify a relation to a norm, to align properly. Interestingly, there is one English usage of "justify" which is very similar—the word processor that "justifies" the margins—aligns all the lines of type. In short, to justify is to rectify the relation to the norm; justification is rectification.

(d) It is one thing to speak of human relationships to a norm, but what does it mean to speak of the "righteousness of God"? By what norm is God to be judged? and who is the judge of the matter? Or does "righteousness of God" mean something quite different from the righteousness of a person? The meaning of "righteousness of God," especially in Paul, has been debated vigorously in recent years. On the surface, the debate has been over a grammatical point—how to take "of." But the issues at stake are far-reaching.

Ernst Käsemann has challenged Bultmann's view that the phrase always denotes the righteousness that comes from God to the believer (Käsemann's essay in *New Testament Questions of Today,* 168-82). Romans 10:3, literally translated, reads "for not knowing the righteousness of God, and seeking to establish their own righteousness, they did not submit to the righteousness of God." The RSV renders it "being ignorant of the righteousness *that comes from* God" and the NEB has "they ignore God's way of righteousness." The RSV and Bultmann appear to be supported by Phil. 3:9 where Paul writes of the righteousness that comes from God to the believer, a new right relationship which is granted by God. Käsemann did not dispute this point, but insisted that Rom. 3:25-26 does speak of God's *own* righteousness. Rather than conclude that Paul used the same phrase in two senses, he sought an understanding of the phrase which underlies both. He found it in the OT and in Jewish apocalyptic, where God's righteousness means his rectifying activity vis-à-vis the world. Käsemann's reconstruction of the morphology of this meaning has been criticized; nonetheless, when the dust settles he will be more "justified" than not.

Having oriented ourselves to the major problem of Paul's "righteousness" language, we can now take up the central question, What has the righteousness of God—the moral integrity of God—to do with the rectification of the human relation to God? Here Rom. 3:25-26 is basic, although difficult to translate. The RSV has Paul say that the Christ-event occurred "to show God's righteousness, because in his divine forbearance he had passed over former sins; it was to prove at the present time that he himself is righteous and that he justifies him who has faith in Jesus." Not only does this obscure the fact that "to show" and "to prove" are virtually identical phrases in Greek, but it shifts from "righteous" to "justify" (for reasons noted above). The NEB, on the other hand, gains semantic consistency but jeopardizes the meaning: "to demonstrate his justice . . . to demonstrate his justice now . . . showing that he is both himself just and justifies. . . . " A more exact rendering is: "to demonstrate his rectitude . . . to demonstrate his rectitude . . . so that he might be in the right by rectifying. . . . " The rectitude of God, God's moral integrity, manifests itself in rectifying the relation between God and persons. God's Godhood comes through in justification. God is never more authentically and characteristically God than in rectifying the ungodly.

What sort of God rectifies the godly, the pious, the religious? Such a God would be most self-consistent, would manifest moral integrity, by rewarding the godly, religious folk who kept all the rules. Such a God would be the patron of a religious community, or of an ethnic or racial group. Moreover, a God who rectified the godly would be calculable and controllable, because an achievement-reward system—which this implies—can be manipulated. Then rectification would be in human hands—those would be in right relation to God who made that relation right. Also, a rectifier of the godly who did not punish all the ungodly would treat certain persons or groups as exceptions, as special cases. But then God's moral integrity would be undercut by such a show of favoritism.

What, then, does it mean to believe that God rectifies the ungodly? First, God is not committed to vindicating clients, a group, party, nation, but to making right precisely everyone who is wrongly related to God. Because to be godly is to be like the God we image, each person or group regards God as the vindicator of its values. This makes God the opponent of those we oppose, the ultimate warrant of human power struggles, wars, acts of self-aggrandizement. God's moral integrity is therefore measured by the success of the clients. But if God is the rectifier of the ungodly, then God's moral integrity is measured solely by God's own character and commitments—"his ways are not our ways." If God rectifies the ungodly, then the persons who need rectification are not others, other groups, the outsiders, the enemy, but everyone whose relation to God is not right. If God rectifies the ungodly, then "God shows no partiality" (Rom. 2:11), and is not the God of the Jews only or of any other group (Rom. 3:29). God's wrath is against "*all* ungodliness and wickedness" (Rom. 1:18).

Second, if God rectifies the ungodly, then God exercises sovereignty in freedom. But the freedom of God is not the capacity to be arbitrary, for that would annul moral integrity. Only a righteous God who is free to be faithful by keeping commitments is capable of rectifying the ungodly, because in so doing God's own rectitude becomes effective. Implicit in Paul's insight is the independence of God from all human domestication, the radical otherness of God from all human effort to make God in our image, and the freedom of God to rectify precisely the relation to a wrongly imaged God. A God who cannot do this is really an ideological no-god, a tribal deity of class, race, sex, or power bloc.

Paul's understanding of the righteousness of God who rectifies the ungodly is grounded in Jesus' cross/resurrection, as Rom. 4:25 makes clear: Jesus "was put to death for our trespasses and raised for our justification" (rectification). The discontinuity between the God who justifies the godly clients and the God who rectifies the ungodly is grounded in the fact that God resurrected a Jesus who died under a curse. In Gal. 3:13 Paul quotes Deut. 21:23, "cursed be everyone who hangs on a tree," which he interprets as a reference to the crucifixion. Therefore Christ became "a curse for us"—that is, he died as a cursed man. Because Jesus was executed as one accursed by the law, the resurrection of precisely this Jesus reveals that God's verdict on him cannot be inferred from the cross. Were that the case, God would indeed rectify the godly who put him there in the name of the law, and in the name of law and order. But Jesus' resurrection reveals God's freedom and otherness. Moreover, unless God's resurrecting Jesus was arbitrary (unthinkable to Paul), the resurrection must reveal both God's fidelity to Jesus and God's integrity, despite appearances to the contrary. The fact that the Christ-event occurred in a sinful world shows Paul that God is free to rectify the world and persons in it, and that this rectification does not depend on human readiness, achieved goodness, or self-wrought rectitude but solely on God's grace. Whoever trusts this God is therefore not only rightly related to God (rectified), but must realign every conception of God and of the human condition according to this event.

The Failure of Law

If *anyone* who trusts the God of the gospel is rightly related to God (rectified), then preaching-trusting overcomes the *universal* human dilemma. Otherwise, the Galatians would have been right—trust/faith would be competent only to a certain extent or in limited areas of life, and would need to be supplemented. Moreover, the parity of all persons in trust/faith implies a solidarity in the human predicament, for the same resolution implies the same dilemma. Paul is thoroughly consistent: "There is no distinction; since all have sinned and fall short of the glory of God" (Rom. 3:22–23).

Furthermore, there is a "law of parsimony" in soteriology—the solution goes as far as, but no farther than, the dilemma. If the human plight is essentially ignorance of what one must do, then it is enough to provide knowledge of it; there is no need for an atonement. If we put alongside this consideration another, that the resolution defines the plight, then the question arises: How deeply into the human dilemma does Paul's understanding of salvation penetrate?

The core of the human dilemma is the dual incapacity of law: (*a*) it cannot produce a right relation to God, one of trust/faith, and (*b*) it cannot overcome the tyranny of death—mortality. For Paul, law fails, not because there is something inherently wrong with it (were that the case, the answer would be to get rid of the law) but because it is frustrated by another reality, sin. Because Paul regards death as the "wages of sin" (Rom. 6:23), the human situation is bounded by sin, death, and law—interrelated domains of power.

Romans 5:12–21 became one of the most fateful passages Paul wrote, for it shaped Augustine's doctrine of original sin, in turn restated by Luther and Calvin. Actually, here Paul is less interested in accounting for sin than in showing the surpassing power of salvation. The passage is structured by comparisons of Adam and Christ, and the consequences of their deeds. Behind Paul's discussion of Adam and Christ stand not only Genesis 3 but Jewish interpretations of Adam, which in turn may have been influenced by the ancient myth of the Primal Man (see Robin Scroggs, *The Last Adam*).

According to Rom. 5:12 "sin came into the world through one man and death through sin, and so death spread to all men because all men sinned." The RSV's "because" renders an expression which the Latin translates as *in quo,* and which Augustine took as "in whom" (all persons sinned). Most recent interpreters agree with the RSV; Paul did not teach "In Adam's fall, we sinned all," but rather that ever since Adam everyone sins. Paul shows no interest in the question of how "original sin" (not his phrase) spread. What does interest him is the universality of sin and the parity of all persons with regard to it (Rom. 5:18–21; see also 3:9, 23).

Paul speaks of sin as if it were a person because he regards it as a tyrant with a power-sphere. Although he writes of "trespasses" in order to bring out the concreteness of disobedience, it is sin that interests him, not particular sins or wrongdoings. According to Paul, we do not sin because we are mortal, because mortality generates *Angst* (anxiety), which in turn generates specious mechanisms which are sinful. Rather, we have become subject to death because of sin. Because everyone participates in sin's domain by sinning, everyone is an accomplice in death's tyranny, not an innocent victim, even though death "reigned" as a tyrant (Rom. 5:14, 17, 21). Because the domain of sin and the domain of death are intimately linked, Paul can say that whoever "has died is freed from sin" (Rom. 6:7). To participate in Christ's death, therefore, is to participate in his liberation from death, and hence from sin, because "death no longer has dominion over him" (Rom. 6:9). In the domain of sin and death, sins are a concrete manifestation of a state of bondage; in the domain of Christ, sins manifest an inconsistency in the status. The tension between the "already" and the "not yet" means that one must struggle to be obedient to the Lord of the new domain (Rom. 6:15–22). Therefore whoever participates in Christ's death and expects to share his resurrection-transformation must now consider himself or herself "dead to sin and alive to God in Christ Jesus" (Rom. 6:11). This "considering" is not a pretending that it is true in order to see what happens, but a claiming by faith and obedience the newness and freedom of the New Age. When one struggles against sin on this basis, "sin will have no dominion over you, since you are not under law but under grace" (Rom. 6:14). Christians are not made incapable of sinning (Gal. 6:1); rather, sin no longer is the determinative domain.

Because sin and death entered the world (not just persons; Rom. 8:19–21), they qualified the human situation long before the law of Moses appeared on the scene. Although it was "added because of transgressions" (Gal. 3:19), it could not "make alive"—lead to life-giving rightness before

God (Gal. 3:21). The reason is now clear: the law is heard only by persons in the domain of sin, under the tyranny of sin and death. In this situation, the actual function of the law with respect to God is to make everyone "accountable to God" and, with respect to the self, to produce "knowledge of sin" (Rom. 3:20).

It must not be forgotten that Paul looked back on his pre-Christian life as one which, measured by law, was "blameless" (Phil. 3:6). This means that Paul does not say that the awareness of non-doing, of failure, and of guilt, dogs a person. Rather, awareness that "through the law comes knowledge of sin" is retrospective Christian insight into life under law. One of the illusions of life under law is that one can succeed, especially more than others, as Rom. 2:17–24 makes clear.

Students of Paul, not only Jews, sometimes complain that Paul has misrepresented what Torah meant in Judaism. This is correct, and beside the point, for Paul does not intend to present the Jewish view of the law but his Christian perception of it. Only from the standpoint of life in Christ, in the Spirit, in the New Age, in trust/faith, does the law look like this.

The foregoing observation is crucial for interpreting Rom. 7:7–25. The whole discussion is designed to make it clear that it is not the law that causes sin, that the law and sin are not equatable (Rom. 7:7); rather, "the law is holy, and the commandment is holy and just and good" (v. 12). The ensuing discussion, however, contains several stubborn problems which vex interpreters. (*a*) At v. 7 Paul begins writing "I." How is this "I" to be understood—as a stylistic "I" or autobiographically? (*b*) What is the significance of the change to present tense in v. 14? The two problems are intertwined. On the one hand, if Paul writes autobiographically, and if the tense-shift is to be taken at face value, then he recounts his personal history with the law, up to the present. On the other hand, if the "I" is stylistic, then the subject may be the Adamic self, and the shift to the present tense may also be stylistic—a matter of rhetorical vividness. The crucial issue is whether vv. 14–25 have in view Christian experience or pre-Christian. Augustine, Luther, Calvin, and some more recent commentators have insisted that Paul is probing Christian existence, including his own. Other recent exegetes insist that the "I am sold under sin" (v. 14) cannot refer to the status of the Christian, especially in view of Rom. 6:14 and 8:2. Either way, Paul reasons as a Christian; he does not portray the Jew's self-awareness.

Even if these paragraphs do describe *our* Christian experience with the law, the exegetical question is whether that is what *Paul* was saying. (*a*) Paul begins by exposing how the law functions with reference to sin: the law provoked sin into action, so that "I died" (v. 9). (Since it is difficult to regard "I was once alive apart from the law" as referring to any point in Paul's own life, there is merit in the suggestion that here "I" refers to Adam.) It is sin that perverts the situation so that "the very commandment which promised life proved to be death to me." The real character of sin is disclosed by the way it works through the good (the law). (*b*) Beginning with v. 15, Paul explains the contradiction between what one wills and what one actually does. Again, the point is that "if I do what I do not want [i.e., what is contrary to the law] I agree that the law is good." But then, who is the real doer? Not "I" but this other reality in me, sin. "I am sold under sin." The good does not reside in me, but sin does. (Verse 18 has been mistranslated for centuries as "nothing good dwells in me"; it must be rendered "the good does not dwell in me." Paul is not answering the question, How much good dwells in me? but rather, Does the good dwell within me at all?) (*c*) So persistent is this disparity between intent and result that "I find it to be a law that when I want to do right, evil lies close at hand." In fact, the inner self delights in God's law but yet it is at war with "another law" which resides in one's "members" (organs of the body) because the empirical self (*sōma,* body) is the means through which death and sin exercise influence.

In other words, because the good does not reside in the self, one cannot simply actualize oneself, bring out an inherent goodness—it is not there. The good has rather to be achieved. Yet this cannot be done for the will is vitiated by the power of sin and death. Paul does not blame physicality any more than he blames the law; he insists instead that the problem is sin which perverts everything, including the law (Rom. 8:3). Because sin and death reign over the self that hears the law (even if sin is not activated until one encounters obligation, it is still there), one cannot gain true life— rectitude before God—by doing what the law asks. Hearing the law only makes matters worse. There is only one solution: being set free from this bondage by being transferred to a domain where the Spirit prevails and where Christ is Lord. In that domain the "just requirement of the law" (Rom. 8:4) can be fulfilled precisely because one is "not under the law but under grace" (Rom. 6:14).

Whether Paul unpacks pre-Christian or Christian experience with the law, the analysis itself is grounded in the resolution of the dilemma. Moreover, as Käsemann's commentary on Romans points out, Romans 7 stands as a warning against concluding that the Christian can fare any better with the law as a way of life than the non-Christian. The Christian can do "the just requirement of the law" only by ceasing to live "under the law." Precisely the devout, religious affirmer of the law of God is exposed as being condemned to inevitable failure. Just as the failure of capitalism becomes apparent only to one who ceases to live by it (e.g., a Marxist), and just as the failure of communism becomes apparent to one who abandons it, so the failure of law is evident only to one who is no longer "under the law but under grace." The greatest illusion of all is the idea that those in Christ can play the achiever's game successfully because they are Christians.

The God Who Keeps Faith

The moral integrity of God manifests itself also with regard to the future, the "not yet." Like Abraham, the Christian is fully convinced that God can keep his word (Rom. 4:21). The trustworthiness of God with respect to the completion of what is inaugurated in Christ was axiomatic for Paul; it underlies his view of the two ages, the gift of the Spirit as down-payment and first-fruits, the present reign of Christ, and the hope of Christ's imminent coming. What Paul wrote to the Philippians runs through his entire theological stance: "I am sure that he who began a good work in you will bring it to completion at the day of Jesus Christ" (Phil. 1:6). Paul insists, "God is faithful" (1 Cor. 1:9; 10:13; 2 Cor. 1:18; 1 Thess. 5:24).

Because God keeps faith in accord with the Christ-event, Paul can appropriate the dialectic of the cross/resurrection for his own life and work. First of all, in the face of the coming judgment (1 Cor. 4:12–15; 2 Cor. 5:10; 1 Thess. 5:9–11), Paul has remarkable confidence, for he is already rectified, his relation to God is already right. Since God has invested so much in the work of rectification, God will not bow out now (Rom. 8:31–34). So the coming judgment is not something to be dreaded, but to be looked forward to as an event of vindication (1 Cor. 1:7–9; 15:58; Phil. 1:27–28; 1 Thess. 5:9–11). Paul expects his mission also to be vindicated, and he expressed a certain pride in his congregations insofar as they live by the gospel (Rom. 15:17–21; 2 Cor. 1:13–14; 3:1–3; Phil. 2:14–16; 1 Thess. 2:19–20).

Second, because it is God who will judge (or Christ), Paul is free from the compulsion of seeking approbation now (1 Cor. 4:1–7; 2 Cor. 10:18; 1

Thess. 2:3–6). He urges the same for his readers (Rom. 12:19–21; 14:10–13).

Third, confidence in God also gives Paul a critical distance from himself and his hard experiences. It really does not matter whether he lives or dies, for he belongs to the Lord in any case (Rom. 14:8–9). Paul learned to live with difficulties and successes (Phil. 4:11–13). In fact, lest his hearers conclude that the gospel is powerful when and because he is impressive, Paul deliberately did not shirk appearing to be "weak" so that the Corinthians' response might be directed all the more clearly to God (1 Cor. 2:2–5). He rejected the possibility of proclaiming himself (2 Cor. 4:1–6). The dialectic of the cross/resurrection is the hallmark of authentic ministers of the gospel, who are clay pots for the real treasure (2 Cor. 4:7). So Paul points out that "we are afflicted in every way, but not crushed . . . always carrying in the body the death of Jesus, so that the life of Jesus [resurrection life] may also be manifested in our bodies" (2 Cor. 4:7–12). He does not have to appear as a winner all the time.

Paul emphasizes this point because the "false apostles" who derailed the Corinthians apparently presented themselves as strong (whereas Paul was weak; 2 Cor. 10:10), eloquent (whereas Paul was not an impressive speaker; 2 Cor. 11:6), claiming that they were worthy to be supported financially (whereas Paul took no money from current converts; 2 Cor. 12:13–16). So Paul wrote with sharp irony of *his* manifest achievements: five times thirty-nine lashes, three times beaten with rods, once stoned, all sorts of dangers and deprivations—all of which manifest his weakness (2 Cor. 11:21—12:10). The God who "chose what is weak in the world to shame the strong" (1 Cor. 2:27), who acted salvifically through the weak and vulnerable Jesus answered Paul's prayer for deliverance from a physical affliction, "My grace is sufficient for you, for my power is made perfect in weakness" (2 Cor. 12:7–9). Difficult experiences, which Paul regarded as a way of sharing Christ's sufferings (2 Cor. 1:5; Phil. 3:10–11) taught him to "rely not on ourselves but on God who raises the dead" (2 Cor. 1:9).

A person can write this way only if Jesus' cross/resurrection is the criterion of what God really is. Such a God is faithful also to Paul in precisely the same way as he was to Jesus. That is, the one who did not spare the Son (Rom. 8:32) will not spare Paul sufferings, vulnerability, weakness, or distress either. Yet nothing can separate Paul—or anyone else who trusts this God—from God's love in Christ, not even death (Rom. 8:38–39).

The gospel for which Paul fought so strenuously and passionately is centered in the God who liberated humanity from bondage to sin, death, and law by sending the Son to be born under the law (Gal. 4:4), to be identified with sin (2 Cor. 5:21) and subject to death (Rom. 6:9). For those who believe this, the Christ-event strips away illusions about who God is and who they are.

We have sought to follow Paul's theological pointers to see whether what he saw can be seen again. He did not see everything. Indeed, Paul himself insisted that he saw but dimly and knew but partly (1 Cor. 13:12). But he fought for the integrity of what he knew, confident that "we can do nothing against the truth, but only for the truth" (2 Cor. 13:8).

BIBLIOGRAPHY OF WORKS CITED

Achtemeier, Paul J. *The Quest for Unity in the New Testament Church.* Philadelphia: Fortress Press, 1987.

Allison, Dale C., Jr. "The Pauline Epistles and the Synoptic Gospels: The Pattern of the Parallels." *New Testament Studies* 28 (1982): 1–32.

Badenas, Robert. *Christ the End of the Law. Romans 10.4 in Pauline Perspective.* JSOT Sup. Ser. 10. Sheffield, Eng.: JSOT Press, 1985.

Barrett, C.K. *The First Epistle to the Corinthians.* New York: Harper & Row, 1968.

Bartchy, S. Scott. *Mallon Chrēsai: First-Century Slavery and the Interpretation of 1 Corinthians 7:21.* SBLDS 11. Atlanta: Scholars Press, 1973.

Beker, J. Christiaan. *Paul the Apostle: The Triumph of God in Life and Thought.* Philadelphia: Fortress Press, 1980.

Betz, Hans Dieter. *Galatians.* Hermeneia. Philadelphia: Fortress Press, 1970.

———. *Second Corinthians 8 and 9.* Hermeneia. Philadelphia: Fortress Press, 1985.

Bornkamm, Günther. *Paul.* New York: Harper & Row, 1971.

Bultmann, Rudolf. *Existence and Faith.* Cleveland: World Publishing, Meridian Books, 1960.

———. *Theology of the New Testament.* 2 vols. New York: Charles Scribner's Sons, 1954–55.

Cullmann, Oscar. *Christ and Time: The Primitive Christian Conception of Time and History.* Philadelphia: Westminster Press, 1950.

Dahl, Nils. *Studies in Paul.* Minneapolis: Augsburg Publishing House, 1977.

Deissmann, Adolf. *Paul.* 1912. Reprint. New York: Harper Torchbooks, 1957.

Donfried, Karl P. *The Romans Debate.* Minneapolis: Augsburg Publishing House, 1977.

Doty, William. *Letters in Primitive Christianity.* Philadelphia: Fortress Press, 1973.

Dunn, James D.G. *Christology in the Making.* Philadelphia: Westminster Press, 1980.

Fiorenza, Elisabeth Schüssler. *In Memory of Her: A Feminist Theological Reconstruction of Christian Origins.* New York: Crossroad, 1983.

Furnish, Victor Paul. *The Moral Teaching of Paul.* Nashville: Abingdon Press, 1979.

———. *Theology and Ethics in Paul.* Nashville: Abingdon Press, 1968.

Gaventa, Beverly Roberts. *From Darkness to Light: Aspects of Conversion in the New Testament.* Philadelphia: Fortress Press, 1986.

Hock, Ronald F. *The Social Context of Paul's Ministry: Tentmaking and Apostleship.* Philadelphia: Fortress Press, 1980.

Hultgren, Arland J. *Christ and His Benefits: Christology and Redemption in the New Testament.* Philadelphia: Fortress Press, 1987.

Johnson, Luke T. *The Writings of the New Testament: An Interpretation.* Philadelphia: Fortress Press, 1986.

Käsemann, Ernst. *New Testament Questions of Today.* Philadelphia: Fortress Press, 1969.

―――. *Perspectives on Paul.* Philadelphia: Fortress Press, 1971.

Keck, Leander E. "Paul and Apocalyptic Theology." *Interpretation* 38 (1984): 229–41.

Keck, Leander E., and Victor Paul Furnish. *The Pauline Letters.* Nashville: Abingdon Press, 1984.

MacDonald, Dennis Ronald. *The Legend and the Apostle.* Philadelphia: Westminster Press, 1983.

Malherbe, Abraham J. *Ancient Epistolary Theorists.* Atlanta: Scholars Press, 1988.

―――. *Paul and the Thessalonians: The Philosophic Tradition of Pastoral Care.* Philadelphia: Fortress Press, 1987.

Martin, Ralph. *Carmen Christi.* Cambridge: Cambridge University Press, 1967.

Meeks, Wayne A. *The First Urban Christians: The Social World of the Apostle Paul.* New Haven, Conn.: Yale University Press, 1983.

Munck, Johannes. *Paul and the Salvation of Mankind.* Atlanta: John Knox Press, 1959.

Pagels, Elaine. *The Gnostic Paul: Gnostic Exegesis of the Pauline Letters.* Philadelphia: Fortress Press, 1975.

Richardson, Alan. "Salvation." In *Interpreter's Dictionary of the Bible.* 4:168–81.

Ridderbos, Herman. *Paul.* Grand Rapids: Wm. B. Eerdmans, 1975.

Rubenstein, Richard L. *My Brother Paul.* New York: Harper & Row, 1972; Harper Torchbooks, 1975.

Sanders, E.P. *Paul, the Law, and the Jewish People.* Philadelphia: Fortress Press, 1983.

―――. *Paul and Palestinian Judaism: A Comparison of Patterns of Religion.* Philadelphia: Fortress Press, 1977.

Sandmel, Samuel. *The Genius of Paul.* 1958. Reprint. Philadelphia: Fortress Press, 1979.

Schmithals, Walter. *Gnosticism in Corinth.* Nashville: Abingdon Press, 1971.

―――. *Paul and the Gnostics.* Nashville: Abingdon Press, 1972.

Scroggs, Robin. *Christology in Paul and John.* Philadelphia: Fortress Press, 1988.

―――. *Paul for a New Day.* Philadelphia: Fortress Press, 1977.

―――. *The Last Adam.* Philadelphia: Fortress Press, 1966.

Stanley, David. "Pauline Allusions to the Sayings of Jesus." *Catholic Biblical Quarterly* 23 (1961): 26–39.

Stendahl, Krister. *Paul Among Jews and Gentiles.* Philadelphia: Fortress Press, 1976.

Stowers, Stanley K. *Letter-Writing in Greco-Roman Antiquity.* Philadelphia: Westminster Press, 1986.

Tannehill, Robert. *Dying and Rising with Christ.* Berlin: Töpelmann, 1966.

Theissen, Gerd. *The Social Setting of Pauline Christianity.* Philadelphia: Fortress Press, 1982. (Essays published 1974–75.)

Walker, William O., Jr. "The Burden of Proof in Identifying Interpolations in the Pauline Letters." *New Testament Studies* 33 (1987): 610–18.

White, John L. *Light from Ancient Letters.* Philadelphia: Fortress Press, 1986.

Yarbrough, O. Larry. *Not Like the Gentiles: Marriage Rules in the Letters of Paul.* SBLDS 80. Atlanta: Scholars Press, 1985.

APPENDIX: PAUL'S THEOLOGY IN HISTORICAL CRITICISM

The discussion of "Paul the Problem" (chap. 1) identified certain salient issues in Pauline scholarship, but, apart from passing remarks, provided neither a sketch of the history of scholarship nor more than a compressed statement of certain conclusions presupposed in the ensuing treatment. Even though this essay surveys the field in more detail, it too is a grossly simplified overview of a highly complex and somewhat convoluted story. While dissertations and monographs regularly rehearse the history of research of a particular issue, and occasionally refer to the terrain of modern theological scholarship, no one has written a comprehensive critical history of Pauline scholarship since Albert Schweitzer, whose *Paul and His Interpreters*[1] repays careful reading six decades later. Indeed, such an undertaking may no longer be possible, partly because of the sheer bulk of material involved, and partly because it has become evident that the historical-critical study of Paul cannot be presented properly if it is isolated from the study of early Christianity as a whole, on the one hand, and from modern intellectual history, on the other.

It is not unreasonable to ask why the student of Paul should know the history of scholarship, since it is all too easy to be diverted from Paul to "the problem of Paul." Nonetheless, without minimizing the importance of reading Paul directly, having a general grasp of the course which the study of his theology has taken can make three important contributions to one's reading and understanding.

First, even a rudimentary knowledge of the history of scholarship provides perspective on one's own understanding. Every reader of the Pauline corpus, however defined, "solves" difficulties in order to gain a coherent understanding, be they matters of Paul's vocabulary, sentences, standpoint, or coherence. An elemental grasp of the contours of Pauline scholarship

1. Albert Schweitzer, *Paul and His Interpreters* (London: Adam and Charles Black, 1912).

126

provides a frame of reference for one's own understanding and questions premature conclusions.

Second, because serious readers of Paul also rely on guides, it is useful   2 to be able to place them on a map in order to understand better the assistance they may provide. Increasingly, this is true with regard to historical criticism, with which this essay is concerned. The recent development of other modes of inquiry, primarily the sociological/anthropological and the literary/structuralist, have made it necessary to grasp the nature, significance, and limitations of historical-critical study, which has dominated biblical scholarship for nearly two centuries. The literary/structuralist approach probes the internal dynamic of each text (letter), and delineates its "world"; it seeks to understand how the text "works," irrespective of its external referent (including a principled disregard for the historical accuracy of its subject matter). Historical-critical study, however, attempts to explain Paul by ferreting out as many genetic relationships between Paul and his antecedents as possible, convinced that he is understood best by situating him accurately in his historical context, and by gauging the accuracy of his reports. The sociological/anthropological approach seeks to understand Paul and his communities by reading the texts in light of the behavior of new religious groups (including their leaders) and their dynamics, whether or not such groups have any historical links to each other. Whereas historical-critical study seeks to identify the particular, unique circumstances and factors in order to account for what Paul did and said, the sociological/anthropological approach is interested in typical behavior. These methods are not mutually exclusive, and the future belongs to that approach which proves to be successful in combining them properly. In the meantime, the bulk of the scholarly literature about Paul continues in the historical-critical mode, and its results are assumed also by the newer methods.

Third, even the frustrations experienced by historical criticism's attempts   3 to see Paul in his own time and place actually illumine Paul and his thought. Historical criticism *has* contributed importantly to our understanding of Paul. Scarcely less significant, however, is the obverse: its inability to answer certain questions decisively and permanently. Learning why this has been the case illumines Paul's letters because an important part of knowledge is learning what cannot be known and why this is the case. Consequently, the sketch that follows is both more and less than a success story of historical criticism.

The history of scholarly studies of Paul contains so many fascinating elements that the story could be told in quite different ways. For example, one might present it as a series of responses to German Protestant scholarship, which until recently dominated the field. Or, one could show how the study of Paul, like biblical scholarship as a whole, reflected much wider intellectual currents and theological climates and trends. Or, one could, like Schweitzer, summarize and assess in chronological sequence the contributions of major scholars. None is appropriate to the aims and scope of this essay. Instead, it will first locate five major turning points in order to provide a broad overview of the whole. The bulk of the essay will then show how, and why, certain issues continue to be debated. The focus will be on matters that affect the understanding of Paul's thought, though obviously other questions must be mentioned as well. Some general reflections on the historical-critical study of Paul will conclude the essay.

Five Turning Points

Once the historical-critical study of Scripture had begun in the eighteenth century, the most important turning point in the study of Paul was the work of F. C. Baur in 1831.[2] His vision of what the enterprise required, as well as the conclusions he reached, changed the course of Pauline studies; his work set the agenda of the discipline, prompting his followers to refine and modify his conclusions and others to disprove them. Baur saw that an understanding of Paul which is both historical and critical requires two things: one must situate Paul accurately in the history of the early church, and one must use historical criticism rigorously to determine which of the thirteen letters attributed to Paul in the New Testament are genuinely from Paul. Truly revolutionary, however, was the way he achieved these ends. Instead of first determining which letters are genuine and then correlating this corpus with Acts in order to place Paul in the early church, Baur reversed the procedure: setting Acts aside, he first located Paul in the history of the church, and then used this history to determine which of the letters are genuine and to account for Acts.

2. Ferdinand Christian Baur's pivotal essay, "The Christ-party in the Corinthian Church, The Opposition of Petrine and Pauline Christianity in the Primitive Church, the Apostle Peter in Rome," appeared in the *Tübinger Zeitschrift für Theologie;* it was followed by articles on the Pastoral Epistles (1835) and the Epistle to the Romans (1836). In 1845, he rewrote and expanded these studies, publishing the result as a comprehensive book on Paul. After Baur's death in 1860, his former student, Eduard Zeller, issued a second, edited edition, which was translated into English by A. Menzies as *Paul the Apostle of Jesus Christ, His Life and Work, His Epistles and His Doctrine,* 2 vols. (London: Williams & Norgate, 1876). The quotations from Baur in this essay are from this English edition.

According to Baur, early Christianity was dominated by the conflict between a law-observant Jewish Christianity which looked to Peter, and a slightly later form, spearheaded by Paul, which emphasized freedom from the law. This reading of the first century provided Baur the criteria for making critical judgments about New Testament texts. On the one hand, he accepted as genuine only those letters that clearly reflected this conflict, namely, Romans, 1 and 2 Corinthians, and Galatians; on the other hand, since Acts says virtually nothing about the conflict, Baur concluded that Acts was a deliberate rewriting of early Christian history designed to foster the later reconciliation of the two parties, long after both apostles were dead. Thus Acts ceased to provide the basis for a truly historical understanding of Paul, and became instead a late-second-century tendentious tract. Because Baur's own theology came to be deeply influenced by Hegel's philosophy, it is often said that he simply applied Hegel's dialectic of history to the New Testament, with Peter representing the thesis, Paul the antithesis, and Acts the resolution. Recent study has shown, however, that Baur developed this view of early Christianity before he came under Hegel's influence.

Brilliant and epoch-making though Baur's work was, its result could not stand for long. For one thing, its affinity with Hegelianism tied its fortunes to a philosophy that soon fell into disrepute, leaving the impression that Baur's history was too schematic, too beholden to a theory to be able to deal adequately with evidence. More important, when the evidence was analyzed carefully and independently, there was no trace of the allegedly sustained conflict. Other investigations restored Philippians to the list of genuine letters, as well as 1 Thessalonians (and Philemon).

2. The next turning point came when, shortly before the end of the nineteenth century, the History of Religion School (a customary rendering of the virtually untranslatable *Religionsgeschichtliche Schule*) emerged, and insisted that the decisive factor in the history of early Christianity was its Hellenization, not Baur's intramural conflict. In order to expose Christianity's indebtedness to the religious history of antiquity, this school emphasized the shift from the Palestinian Jewish to the Hellenistic gentile environment. To be sure, scholars had long related the New Testament to authors like Plato or Seneca. The History of Religion School, however, turned to nonliterary materials—newly discovered papyri, inscriptions, esoteric texts, amulets, and so forth—in order to reconstruct the fuller range of Greco-Roman religiosity as the matrix of early Christianity. A truly historical-critical understanding of Paul, therefore, would show the

extent to which his thought, and the form of Christianity in which it was rooted, was largely a particular variant of the religious sensibility of the age, because as Christianity entered the Hellenistic world it became a syncretistic religion in an age of syncretism.[3] In order to support such a claim, classicists and New Testament scholars identified Hellenistic ideas, myths, motifs, and practices that appear comparable to those in early Christianity, and traced their histories as far back as possible. Thus "parallels" became "antecedents," which in turn became "influences" or, more simply, evidence of a shared religious sensibility.

Although the evidence was derived from widely scattered sources, scholars reconstructed particular religions like Mithraism and various but similar mystery religions, whose secret initiatory rites promised participation in the immortality of the gods.[4] In the early years of this century, it was sometimes argued that these mystery religions explained the rapid spread of Christianity because "many of the Greeks must have regarded Christianity as a superior form of 'Mystery Religion.' "[5] This view of the Hellenization of Christianity, however, could not survive the growing evidence that the heyday of the Mysteries came long after Paul, and the realization that, as Schweitzer put it, "Paulinism . . . is a theological system with sacraments, not a Mystery-religion."[6] Still, one can scarcely deny that common to Paul (and Hellenistic Christianity) and the Mysteries was the assumption that sacred rites did make one a participant in a divine savior figure; 1 Cor. 10:16–23 is quite unintelligible otherwise.

The most influential—and most controversial—claim of the history of religion enterprise has been that the key to early Christianity was Gnosticism, which had been regarded as a Christian heresy of the second century. Adolf Harnack had given Gnosticism a more positive role by regarding the gnostic leaders as the first theologians who systematized the tradition (while rejecting the Old Testament), and who "attempted to capture Christianity for Hellenic culture, and Hellenic culture for Christianity." Hence

---

3. This was the point of Hermann Gunkel's book which showed the significance of the history of religion approach, *Zum religionsgeschichtlichen Verständnis des Neuen Testaments* (Göttingen: Vandenhoeck & Ruprecht, 1905), 95.

4. See, e.g., the magisterial studies of the Belgian scholar Franz Cumont, *The Mysteries of Mithra* (1st ed. 1900; 2d ed. trans. 1902; reprint, New York: Dover Publications, 1956); *Oriental Religions in Roman Paganism* (1906; reprint, New York: Dover Publications, 1956).

5. Kirsopp Lake, *The Earlier Epistles of St. Paul* (London: Rivington's, 1914), 45.

6. Schweitzer, *Paul and His Interpreters*, 215. So too H. A. A. Kennedy concluded that "the background and atmosphere of the Pauline conceptions of death and resurrection with Christ are so incongruous with the Mystery-religions as to rob of their validity any parallels that may be adduced." *St. Paul and the Mystery Religions* (London: Hodder and Stoughton, 1913), 230.

Gnosticism was the "acute secularising or hellenising of Christianity."[7] The history of religion scholars went farther, and saw it as an independent, pre-Christian religious movement which influenced Christianity almost from the start. For this understanding of Gnosticism, they relied on quite different evidence, such as the literature of the Mandaeans (an anti-Christian, anti-Jewish sect still found in southern Iraq), certain Manichean texts (the Turfan fragments found in Chinese Turkestan), and the Egyptian Hermetic writings—none of which are pre-Christian but which, it was claimed, represent ideas from pre-Christian times.[8] The discovery, in 1945, of a Coptic "gnostic" library at Nag Hammadi, Egypt,[9] has compounded the difficulty of defining Gnosticism because these texts from the Christian era are also highly diverse and represent different degrees of Christian influence. It is not surprising that questions of the definition, nature, origin, and possible influence of Gnosticism have been debated vigorously.[10]

Especially important has been the claim that one could recover a widespread theology of salvation made possible by a cosmic figure, the redeemed Redeemer, who appeared on earth to bring saving knowledge (*gnosis*) to those able to receive it. The redeemer myth too was constructed out of widely disparate materials, partly from the Christian era and partly from earlier times. Hellenistic Christianity, including Paul, was said to have appropriated this myth, though not all of its view of salvation, in order to interpret the identity and significance of Jesus. Here too, careful examination of the evidence has shown that the redeemer myth is largely a

7. Adolf Harnack, *History of Dogma* (1st German ed. 1885; trans. 3d ed., London: Williams & Norgate, 1905), 227–28. Today, neither the old view of Gnosticism as a Christian heresy nor Harnack's modification is defended.

8. For a convenient, critical survey of the history of research, see Edwin Yamauchi, *Pre-Christian Gnosticism: A Survey of Proposed Evidences* (Grand Rapids: Wm. B. Eerdmans, 1973). The most convenient selection of primary sources is Werner Foerster, *Gnosis*, 2 vols. (Oxford: Clarendon Press, 1972, 1974).

9. Coptic "gnostic" library texts are available in English: *The Nag Hammadi Library*, ed. James M. Robinson (New York/San Francisco: Harper & Row, 1977); *The Gnostic Scriptures*, trans., annotated, and introduced Bentley Layton (New York: Doubleday & Co., 1987).

10. For the problem of definition, see Kurt Rudolf, " 'Gnosis' and 'Gnosticism'—The Problems of Definition and Their Relation to the Writings of the New Testament," *The New Testament and Gnosis*, R. Mcl. Wilson Festschrift, ed. A. H. B. Logan and A. J. M. Wedderburn (Edinburgh: T. & T. Clark, 1983), 21–37. See also Morton Smith, "The History of the Term Gnostikos," in *The Rediscovery of Gnosticism*, ed. Bentley Layton (Leiden: E. J. Brill, 1981), II:796–807. Smith's skepticism about the reconstructions of Gnosticism, based on heterogeneous evidence (including the tendentious polemics of "orthodox" church fathers), is expressed in his tart observation that "the term 'gnosticism' has become in effect a brand name with a secure market. 'Gnosticism' is salable, therefore it will continue to be produced. Indeed, our lack of information about true, ancient gnosticism will probably prove a great advantage to manufacturers of the modern, synthetic substitute" (807).

modern construct which cannot be documented in the form in which enthusiastic scholars have often presented it.[11] But again, it is difficult to deny that even if a complete myth cannot be found in pre-Christian sources, the general mythic pattern, with many variations, was assumed in Paul's day, and that it seems to account for certain aspects of his Christology—and that of John's Gospel as well.

No single book produced by the History of Religion School has been more influential than Wilhelm Bousset's *Kyrios Christos,* originally published in 1913 but not translated into English until 1970.[12] Its subtitle describes the content: "The History of the Belief in Christ from the Beginning of Christianity to Irenaeus" (i.e., until 200 C.E.). Bousset sharply contrasted the earliest Christianity in Palestine, whose apocalyptic orientation focused on the expected coming of Jesus as the Son of Man, and Hellenistic gentile Christianity, a Spirit-filled community that worshiped Jesus as the present *Kyrios* (Lord), a title first given to Jesus by Hellenistic gentile Christians. When Bousset described these *Kyrios*-communities in places like Antioch, his imagination soared:

> Around the *Kyrios* the community is gathered in believing reverence, it confesses his name, under the invocation of his name it baptizes, it assembles around the table of the Lord Jesus; it sighs in the fervent cry, "Maranatha, come, Lord Jesus"; . . . under the invocation of his name people perform miracles and drive demons out! . . . They come together in the evening, probably as often as possible for the common sacred meal. There they experienced the miracle of fellowship, the glow of the enthusiasm of a common faith and a common hope; there the spirit blazed high, and a world full of wonders surrounded them; prophets and those who speak in tongues, visionaries and ecstatic persons begin to speak; psalms, hymns, and spiritual songs sound through the room, the powers of brotherly kindness come alive. . . . And over this whole swaying sea of inspiration reigns the Lord Jesus . . . with his power immediately present and breathtaking palpable presence and certainty. (134–5)

Not surprisingly, in contrasting earlier apocalyptic Christianity with that of the *Kyrios,* Bousset can write: "Out of a religion of the future and of pure yearning develops a religion of blessed fulfillment and certainty" (198). Out of this religion Paul formed a more individualized, more ethical mysticism. Even so, his religious experience of the Lord virtually eclipsed

11. In his discussion of "Gnostic Motifs" (in early Christianity), Rudolf Bultmann summarized the reconstructed myth. *Theology of the New Testament* (New York: Charles Scribner's Sons, 1954), I:164–83, esp. 166–67.

12. Wilhelm Bousset, *Kyrios Christos* (Nashville: Abingdon Press, 1970). All page references are to this edition.

his theology; when Bousset turned to Paul's thought, he commented on the impact of Christ's exalted role on monotheism, but said not a word about the law and Israel, and justification is barely mentioned; though the Lord is the center, Bousset says virtually nothing about Paul's Christology.

This book, which synthesized Bousset's enormous learning, became very influential, especially in Germany, because it brought to bear on the early history of Christianity the materials assembled by the History of Religion School, and did so in a way that provided an overall, plausible account. Though eroded at many points by the ongoing research, especially with regard to the origin of the worship of Jesus as the *Kyrios*,[13] it too shaped the agenda of the future. In fact, Rudolf Bultmann relied on Bousset's distinction between Palestinian and later Hellenistic (gentile) Christianity to distinguish earlier and later elements of the Synoptic tradition, without which his form-criticism of the Gospel materials can scarcely be imagined. Likewise, Bultmann's *New Testament Theology* rests squarely on Bousset's framework. The current sociological/anthropological approach can be regarded as carrying out with more precision what Bousset pioneered: understanding early Christianity, and so Paul as well, as a socioreligious phenomenon of Greco-Roman culture.

3. Because the history of religion approach championed Hellenization as the leitmotif of early Christianity, the discovery of the apocalyptic factor[14] deserves to be regarded as the third turning point, for this provided a significant alternative reconstruction—at least in the thinking of Schweitzer, its most ardent advocate. Formally, of course, the history of religion approach is as concerned to explore the role of Jewish apocalyptic as that of Hellenism, and seeks to determine the relative importance of each. In fact, however, Bousset was one of the very few scholars with sufficient mastery of the sources in both fields to be able to do this. Most scholars worked primarily in one domain or the other; inevitably each group cham-

13. See, e.g., Ferdinand Hahn, "Kyrios," in *The Titles of Jesus in Christology* (New York/Cleveland: World Publishing, 1969), chap. 2; Joseph A. Fitzmyer, S.J., "New Testament *Kyrios* and *Maranatha* and Their Aramaic Background," in *To Advance the Gospel* (New York: Crossroad, 1981), 218–35.

14. Although a few mid-nineteenth-century German scholars had called attention to the role of Jewish apocalyptic thought, it was Johannes Weiss who appears to have put the cat among the pigeons in 1892 with his *Jesus' Proclamation of the Kingdom of God*, trans. and ed. Richard Hiers and D. Larrimore Holland; Lives of Jesus (Philadelphia: Fortress Press, 1971); Klaus Koch, *The Rediscovery of Apocalyptic*, Studies in Biblical Theology II, 22 (Naperville, Ill.: Alec R. Allenson, 1974) is both a history of research and a vigorous critique of the consequences of neglecting apocalyptic.

pioned the significance of its material—giving the impression that one must choose between "Hellenizers" and "Judaizers."

Also involved was the theological import of historical continuity/discontinuity. The history of religion schema emphasized discontinuities where Christian theology had predicated continuities: between a Jesus who did not regard himself as the Messiah and whose message was congenial with ethical idealism, and earliest Jewish Christianity which regarded him as Messiah and coming Son of Man in accord with its general apocalyptic character; and between this earliest Christianity and Hellenistic Christianity, whether inaugurated by Paul or propagated by him. Such a Christianity created enormous theological problems because it would have been in effect a new religion, severed from both the earliest church and Jesus. Schweitzer rejected this sharply: according to the History of Religion School, "Paulinism ought to be detached from early Christianity and closely connected with Greek theology. The contrary is the case. It stands in undisturbed connection with the former, whereas it shows no connexion whatever with the latter."[15] Accordingly, Schweitzer argued for continuity between Jesus, earliest Christianity, and Paul—a continuity grounded in the Jewish apocalyptic theology they all shared. At the same time, the continuity found by Schweitzer had an unwelcome effect: although this implied that the Hellenization of Christianity came after Paul, it located the real issue that dominated its early years in the event that did not happen—"the Second Coming" of Christ. That is, making apocalyptic central to the continuity between Jesus, earliest Christianity, and Paul invited embarrassment because the imminent coming of the Lord proved to be a mistaken conviction.

The twin offspring of the history of religion approach—the "Hellenizers" and the "Judaizers" (which came to include types of Judaism other than apocalyptic)—have contended with one another repeatedly, like Jacob and Esau. Neither group gave due recognition to the complexity of the ancient world, or saw clearly enough the role of a mediating factor— Hellenistic Jewish Christianity.[16] Nevertheless, between them they exposed the degree to which Paul's thought was at home in a world fundamentally different from our own.

---

15. Schweitzer, *Paul and His Interpreters*, 230.
16. The first major work that identified as clearly as possible the characteristic Christology of Hellenistic Jewish Christianity was Hahn's *Titles of Jesus in Christology* (see n. 10).

4. The fourth turning point was signaled by the work of Bultmann, in whose hands virtually the entire historical-critical study of the New Testament achieved its most powerful expression,[17] for it combined the history of religion approach with a theological stance generally consonant with its most trenchant critique—that of Karl Barth's early work immediately after World War I. That slaughter had reduced to shambles much that liberal Protestantism had stood for—optimism about the human capacity to know God (whether on the basis of history, logic, or innate religious sensibility), and to create a Christian civilization on the basis of Christianity's best ideals. Barth, inspired by Kierkegaard (recently translated into German), insisted that there is no bridge from the human to the divine because the infinite qualitative distinction between them precludes this. Because religion is nothing other than the human effort to bridge the unbridgeable, knowledge of God depends on revelation, "from beyond." Nor is God an object of thought and inquiry by the human subject; rather God is the subject, whose Word interprets all human hope and despair alike. It is not God who is the problem, but the human self and human knowledge/arrogance.

Barth did not deny the right of historical criticism, including the history of religion enterprise, to reconstruct the circumstances under which the New Testament came into being, but he was not impressed by the "parallels" between the emergent Christian religion and the religions of the day, for insofar as Christianity became a religion it too became a human enterprise; what he did deny was that God's act in Christ could be understood rightly as a religion at all. Thus the results of historical-critical work were theologically unimportant. Barth's revolution-making commentary on Romans,[18] therefore, did not explain where Paul got his ideas or how they were related to comparable ideas of the day. Rather, it undertook to make sense of Paul's theology on the assumption that the apostle was right: God's act in Christ confronts the whole world with a crisis-inducing No in order

---

17. See the excellent brief introduction to Bultmann's work by Norman Perrin, *The Promise of Bultmann* (Philadelphia: Fortress Press, 1979). For a thorough exposition of Bultmann's work and thought, see Walter Schmithals, *An Introduction to the Theology of Rudolf Bultmann* (Minneapolis: Augsburg Publishing House, 1968). Schmithals eschews making his own assessment of Bultmann.

18. Karl Barth published three commentaries on Romans. The first was published in 1918. The second, published in 1921, rewrote the first completely, and, with minor revisions, was reissued repeatedly until the sixth edition (1928). The third, originally a popular lecture course in 1940–41, appeared in English as *A Shorter Commentary on Romans* (Richmond: John Knox Press, 1956). It is the second commentary of 1921, together with all prefaces through the sixth edition, that the English-using world knows best, *The Epistle to the Romans* (London: Oxford University Press, 1933).

to offer a salvific Yes so drastic that it could only be believed. Truly salvific faith is a risk-taking response to God's Word, which is not a thing (e.g., a book) but an event in which one's existence is dissolved and reconstituted at the same time.

Bultmann agreed. The subject matter of theology is not experience (whether religious experience or human achievement in culture) but God—the God who "represents the total annulment of man," whose "fundamental sin is his will to justify himself as man," thereby making himself God.[19] At the same time, however, he combined Barthian Word of God theology and the history of religion approach. Indeed, in New Testament circles, he became the most influential history of religion scholar since Bousset, whose work he refined. Agreeing that the Hellenization of Christianity was the decisive factor, he emphasized the influence of Gnosticism on the Hellenistic gentile Christianity in which Paul's theology was rooted. What was unique in Christianity was the claim that God had acted in Christ, an actual historical person.[20] Moreover, he appropriated Hans Jonas's interpretation of Gnosticism, which relied on Heideggerian existentialism to penetrate the diverse gnostic mythologies in order to expose a common self-understanding: the self as alien in the world, called to authentic existence by the redeemed Redeemer.[21]

Equipped with this mode of reading ancient religious texts, all of which assume a mythological world view, Bultmann recast both gnostic mythology and New Testament theology into existentialist categories, so that despite differences in vocabulary what came to light was remarkably a similar self-understanding. It is this that the Word of God, centered in the kerygma, the proclamation of God's act in Jesus' cross/resurrection, reconstitutes when it is believed. Like Barth, Bultmann insisted that the Word

19. Rudolf Bultmann, "Liberal Theology and the Latest Theological Movement," in *Faith and Understanding*, ed. R.W. Funk (New York and Evanston: Harper & Row, 1969), 28–52, esp. 46.

20. Rudolf Bultmann, *Primitive Christianity* (New York: World Publishing, Meridian Books, 1956), 200. Bultmann immediately qualifies this uniqueness by saying that "it would be wrong to lay too much stress on this," partly because the "historical person of Jesus was very soon turned into a myth," and partly because also the Gnostics believed that "the advent of the redeemer was a real event and the source of the tradition enshrined in their worship and doctrine." What really distinguishes Christianity is its anthropology: whereas for the Gnostics salvation is the liberation of the eternal essence from matter, for the Christian faith it is the emancipation of the self from a guilty past so that one can have an authentic existence as a deciding self (see 202).

21. Hans Jonas, *The Gnostic Religion* (Boston: Beacon Press, 1958), is a good summary of the earlier work that influenced Rudolf Bultmann, *Gnosis und spätantiker Geist,* 2 vols. (Göttingen: Vandenhoeck & Ruprecht, 1934, 1954).

of God has no credentials that the hearer can check before responding in faith; it is a self-authenticating event that elicits a Yes or No. Unlike Barth, he translated Christian theology into anthropology, which he "demythologized" into the structure of the existence of the believing self.[22] An encyclopedia article on Paul, published in 1930,[23] anticipates the magisterial section on Paul in the *Theology of the New Testament*, published in 1948.[24] For a time, subsequent interpretations of Paul had to come to terms with Bultmann's work.

(5.) Because until now no overarching interpretation of Paul has replaced Bultmann's, the fifth turning point can be spoken of as the disintegration of the Bultmannian synthesis. Although this is so near to our time that it is difficult to get proper perspective on it, it is possible to identify factors that brought its enormous influence into a swift and sharp decline. The most important rupture in the synthesis came from within the circle of Bultmann's students, namely, from the work of Ernst Käsemann, which will be noted later. At this point it suffices to say that he denied that Paul's theology can be reduced to anthropology because its center emphasizes God's own righteousness as the divine movement in Christ to reclaim sovereignty over creation (not simply over deciding selves), and that this apocalyptic dimension must be acknowledged.

External factors were no less important, especially on the American scene, beginning with the fact that Bultmann's philosophical underpinning—existentialism—swiftly lost its appeal in the face of the societal upheavals of the late 60s. It was too individualistic, given the rapid rise of concern for redemption *of* the world (issues of social justice, peace, human rights, ecology, etc.); Bultmann's construal of salvation as liberation *from* the "world" (*Entweltichung*) was swept away by the revived liberal Protestant (and now Catholic as well) passion to change the world. Moreover, the whole Barthian-Bultmannian understanding of the Word of God lost its viability once the experience of hearing this Word dissipated, for this understanding was an answer to questions the next generation did not acknowledge as its own. In addition, the literary and sociologi-

---

22. Rudolf Bultmann, "New Testament and Mythology," in *Kerygma and Myth: A Theological Debate,* ed. H.W. Bartsch (New York: Harper & Row, 1961), 1–44. Bultmann asserted that Christ "meets us in the word of preaching and nowhere else," and that this word "confronts us in the word of God. It is not for us to question its credentials" (41).

23. Rudolf Bultmann, "Paul," in *Existence and Faith* (New York: World Publishing, Meridian Books, 1960), 111–46.

24. Bultmann, *Theology of the New Testament,* I:185–352.

cal/anthropological approaches to texts appeared to promise access to Paul that was less beholden to explicitly Christian categories and concerns.

Persistent Issues

The historical-critical study of the theology of Paul, as of any significant figure, requires a judicious use of sound methods, a plausible historical reconstruction of circumstances and influences, and the capacity to enter the apostle's thought sufficiently to be able to communicate it. Not all scholars combine a high degree of competence in all three areas. Moreover, they are as subject to historical circumstances and influences as he was; they too respond to issues on the minds of the readers, engage opponents, and defend their convictions—not infrequently resorting to polemics in doing so. Above all, one must always remember that the magnitude of the historical task is not proportionate to the amount of material with which to work; using a few pages of edited letters, one is to grasp the thought of a seminal mind in such a way that its relations to Christian predecessors and contemporaries (mostly unknown) as well as to its cultural context (documented only fragmentarily) are brought into proper perspective. In such an enterprise, everything affects everything else, as when one adjusts a mobile. It is not surprising, then, that few indeed are the questions that are answered permanently, and that many refuse to be silenced for long.

Two major efforts are especially important in the study of Paul's theology: one attempts to account historically for Paul's theology by tracing genetic relationships and "causes" in order to explain; the other attempts to grasp the content of Paul's thought as theology by seeking coherences in order to understand. Clearly, they can be distinguished but not really separated.

Accounting for Paul's Thought Historically

The many attempts to account historically (i.e., explain) for Paul's theology can be divided into two groups. The first has emphasized Paul's context, whether cultural or Christian, or both. It sought to explain his thought in the letters by looking outside them, by appealing to the influence of Hellenism, either direct or indirect through the Hellenistic Christianity Paul represented. This appeal to external factors was used to account for the *polemical* character of much of Paul's theology. The second group has emphasized Paul himself, his personal experience and religious consciousness. It sought to explain his thought in the letters by looking behind them, by reconstructing his unique spiritual biography, often emphasizing his Jewish heritage, in order to account for the highly *personal* character of his thought. Neither of these approaches ignores the other completely, of course.

Undoubtedly, the *polemical* character of Paul's thought reflects his struggles with opponents. Baur overemphasized opposition to Paul from law-observant Jewish Christianity centered in Jerusalem; given Paul's own words in Galatians 1–2 and Rom. 15:22–32 as well as his experience in Jerusalem according to Acts 21:17–36, it is difficult to deny outright that there was significant tension. Johannes Munck,[25] however, did just that, arguing that for Paul Christianity is true Judaism and the church the true Israel, Jerusalem the center of the world, and Israel's conversion the most important event before the *Parousia* (the "coming"), which Paul's mission to the Gentiles was designed to provoke. On the whole, Munck's reconstruction is as lopsided and unconvincing as was Baur's. So the question remained: Can one reconstruct the relation between Jerusalem Christianity and Paul?

The discovery of the Dead Sea Scrolls in 1947 raised hopes that this could be done, for these texts stimulated an intensive study of Jewish Christianity—including a debate over whether that designation itself is appropriate.[26] Achieving a reliable picture of Paul's relationship to Jerusalem Christianity has proved to be extraordinarily difficult because there are no texts from its representatives; one must work backwards not only from Paul (who provides the earliest evidence) but also from later memories, traditions, legends, polemics contained in literature ranging from the last decades of the first century (Acts) to the fourth century (Epiphanius). It is not surprising that a commonly accepted, comprehensive account of early Christianity in its homeland before 70 C.E. has not yet been produced, though all sorts of reconstructions have been proposed. What has become clear, however, is that early Christianity was highly diverse, and probably given to contentiousness and fragmentation as well—what one expects of a movement with relatively little structure and enormous energy.

25. Johannes Munck, *Paul and the Salvation of Mankind* (London: SCM Press, 1959). Munck declared flatly, "No conflict existed between Jewish Christianity and Paul" (279).

26. See, e.g., Robert A. Kraft, "In Search of 'Jewish Christianity' and Its 'Theology': Problems of Definition and Methodology," in *Judeo-Christianisme*, Jean Danielou Festschrift (Paris: Editions Beauchesne, 1972 [also published as *Recherches de Science Religieuse* 60 (1972): 1–320]), 81–92; A. F. J. Klijn, "The Study of Jewish Christianity," *New Testament Studies* 20 (1974): 419–31; Stanley K. Riegel, "Jewish Christianity: Definitions and Terminology," *New Testament Studies* 24 (1978): 410–15.

Because it has proven to be virtually impossible to achieve a broad consensus about Paul's relation to earliest Christianity, important questions receive widely disparate answers: What beliefs about Jesus gave this movement its shape? What roles did Peter, James, and Stephen (who is not mentioned by Paul but is important for Acts) really play? What form of Christianity did Paul persecute, and why did he do so? What relation, if any, was there between Jerusalem and the "Judaizers" in Galatia? Why was Paul apprehensive lest Jerusalem not accept the offering for the poor (Rom. 15:22–32)? Without firm answers to such questions, attempts to account for the polemical character of Paul's theology by appealing to opposition in Jerusalem must remain unconvincing.

For the "Hellenizers" of the history of religion approach, the decisive resistance to Paul did not come from Palestine but either from local misconstruals of his thought or from traveling Christian teachers who appeared in his congregations while he was absent. Once one ceases to hold Jerusalem Christianity responsible for Paul's opposition in his own churches, the door is open for all sorts of other proposals because there are no external controls for identifying them or for reconstructing their criticism of Paul; everything must be inferred from Paul's own polemical responses to them. Consequently, scholarly creativity has populated Paul's churches with diverse persons, groups, and tendencies. According to John J. Gunther's account,[27] scholars found nine different opponents in Galatia, ranging from local Judaizing Gentiles to libertine gnostic Jewish Christians; in Philippi they found twenty-five, ranging from non-Christian Jews to proselytes to Judaizers to Jewish gnostic perfectionists with radicalized spiritualistic eschatology—all predicated on the basis of Paul's polemic in Philippians 3. Dieter Georgi's recently translated monograph on Paul's opponents in 2 Corinthians is the high-water mark of such reconstructions,[28] most of which are monuments to the historical imagination of their authors.

Nonetheless, several things deserve to be remembered. (*a*) The need to develop a profile of Paul's opposition derives from the nature of the letters themselves, which Paul wrote in order to contend for his understanding of the gospel in the face of distortions of it being advocated in his churches. Paul did not write because he felt he owed it to his constituency to express

---

27. John J. Gunther, *St. Paul's Opponents and Their Background* (Leiden: E.J. Brill, 1973), 1–2.

28. Dieter Georgi, *The Opponents of Paul in Second Corinthians* (Philadelphia: Fortress Press, 1986).

himself more fully on papyrus; nor did he initiate criticisms of other Christian teachers like Peter or Barnabas. He wrote because he became convinced that the truth of the gospel was being threatened. (*b*) It is by no means obvious that these distortions were always generated by outsiders, or that they all were variants of a single tendency, whether Baur's Judaizers or Walter Schmithals's Hellenistic Jewish gnostic Christians, which he finds everywhere.[29] It is more likely that the issues differed from place to place, and that in a given place like Corinth or Philippi they changed rapidly. (*c*) One should be wary of simply reversing Paul in order to recover the thought of his opposition, because Paul often transposed the categories in order to put his response on a different level. In 1 Corinthians 6—7 he refuses to be drawn into a speculative discussion of "sexuality and spirituality" (which the Corinthians probably wanted) and instead transposed the discussion "downward" onto the pragmatic level; in Romans 14—15, on the other hand, he transposed the discussion of religiously sanctioned days and diets "upward" into broader considerations, including the astounding generalization, "Whatever does not proceed from the faith is sin" (14:23). On the other hand, in 2 Corinthians 10—12, where he uses the opponents' weakness/strength language, he pointedly does so in an ironic mode in order to undermine their views from within. (*d*) Paul's skill as a polemicist and his capacity to respond in differing ways to diverse situations produced the diverse accents in his letters. Not surprisingly, scholars have sometimes wondered whether he was a coherent thinker (see below).[30]

Others have accounted for Paul's theology by regarding it as the expression of his *unique personal history.* To do so entails, first of all, discerning how he dealt with the Pharisaism he had advocated (Phil. 3:5). Here too the nature of the evidence makes the task formidable: between Pharisaism as Paul had known it and the earliest rabbinic texts stands the virtual transformation of Judaism as the result of two revolts against Rome (66-70;

2.

---

29. See Walter Schmithals's essays in *Paul and the Gnostics* (Nashville: Abingdon Press, 1972).

30. Percy Gardner declared, "Paul is seldom free from inconsistency. In his fervid brain, points of view succeeded one another as he dictated, and at the moment each filled the spaces in his mind and seemed the sum of the truth. He did not turn back to see what he had written before, nor stop to think whether he was going too far in the statement of a particular doctrine." *The Religious Experience of St. Paul* (London: Williams & Norgate, 1911), 161-62. More recently, Heikki Räisänen concluded his study of Paul's view of the law by saying, "In sum, I am not able to find in the relevant literature *any* conception of the law which involves such inconsistencies or such arbitrariness as does Paul's." *Paul and the Law* (Philadelphia: Fortress Press, 1986), 228.

132–135 C.E.). The oral traditions compiled after the Second Revolt reflect the standpoint of the rabbinate, which muted what was not congenial to its perspectives, especially apocalyptic. Nonetheless, because traditions had been transmitted with considerable care, it is possible to work backward into the pre-70 period, but few Christian scholars have been equipped linguistically to do this, and a Protestant prejudice against legalism and ritualism (read "Roman Catholicism") also made it easier to avoid the rabbinic than the Greek sources.

One of the most influential attempts to account for Paul's theology by appealing to his Pharisaic heritage was that of W. D. Davies, who contended that Paul was "primarily governed both in life and in thought by Pharisaic concepts, which he had baptized 'unto Christ.' "[31] In Davies's hands, "rabbinic Judaism" has considerable elasticity, for he not only refused to differentiate it sharply from other types of Judaism (especially apocalyptic) but declined to contrast it sharply with Hellenism as well. This approach has largely been vindicated. More problematic is his procedure: he finds sufficient similarity between certain of Paul's themes and ideas and their Jewish counterparts to claim that it is unnecessary to look elsewhere to account for their presence in Paul. Thus Jewish speculations about Adam suffice to account for Paul's cosmic Christ, making it unnecessary to refer to the gnostic myth of the Redeemer, who was called Anthropos. Paul is not only deeply dependent on the Jesus-tradition, but construed Christ as having taken the place of the Torah. Moreover, since Paul regarded Christianity as "the advent of the true and final form of Judaism," justification by faith is not at all its "quintessence."[32]

Davies's student, E. P. Sanders,[33] undertook to dismantle much of what Davies had tried to construct. Not only did Sanders differentiate various types of Judaism in Palestine, but he insisted that both Judaism and Christianity must be grasped systemically, as two essentially different types of religion (543). On this basis, Davies's procedure of comparing themes and ideas missed the point. The key to Paul's theology is not his Jewish heritage at all but his exclusivist view of salvation as centered only in Christ (519).

31. W. D. Davies, *Paul and Rabbinic Judaism*, 4th ed. (1st ed. 1948; Philadelphia: Fortress Press, 1980), 16. The 4th ed. contains "Paul and Judaism since Schweitzer," a review of Schoeps's *Paul*, and an assessment of E. P. Sanders's *Paul and Palestinian Judaism* (see below).

32. Davies, *Paul and Rabbinic Judaism*, 324, 222.

33. E. P. Sanders, *Paul and Palestinian Judaism: A Comparison of Patterns of Religion* (Philadelphia: Fortress Press, 1977).

Sanders rightly sees that Paul's thought moves from solution to plight, not the reverse. This leads him to conclude that what Paul finds wrong with Judaism is that "*it is not Christianity*" (552, italics his). In short, the pattern of Paul's "thought cannot be explained satisfactorily as having been derived from Palestinian Judaism" (552–3). Although Sanders is probably right in denying that Paul's theology is essentially refocused Judaism, the book is finally unsatisfying because it does not clarify what Paul does owe to Pharisaism, or to put it differently, what difference it made in Paul's theology that he had been a "Pharisee of the Pharisees" before he became an apostle of Jesus Christ. That entails seeing discontinuities as well as continuities, and venturing to account for both. Doing that, however, leads one to consider what both Davies and Sanders—as well as many others—avoided: Paul's conversion.

Emphasizing his conversion has scarcely fared better, though sometimes the claims have been far from modest. Paul's conversion was emphasized over a century ago, but subsequently many scholars declined to deal with it, partly because, given the scant data, they regarded it as a futile exercise, and partly because on this point some German Protestant scholarship was allergic to "psychologism." Recently, however, the Korean scholar Seyoon Kim has reasserted the decisive significance of Paul's Damascus road experience.[34]

Those who regard Paul's conversion as the key to his theology do not have much evidence with which to work. On the one hand, they must correlate properly Paul's theologically formulated allusions to the event (e.g., Rom. 1:5; Gal. 1:11–16), in which conversion and commission to preach to the Gentiles coincide, with the three descriptions in Acts (9:1–19; 22:3–16; 26:9–18) where conversion and commission coincide only in the third account. On the other hand, they must clarify the relation between what Paul opposed as persecutor and what he advocated as propagator of the gospel, and do so in a way that is as plausible theologically as it is psychologically.

The course of the debate exposes the issues, beginning with the accounts in Acts, which agree that Paul's conversion resulted from a vision of Christ. Carl Holsten[35] argued that what Paul saw was Christ as the Second Adam,

34. Seyoon Kim, *The Origin of Paul's Gospel*, WUNT 114 (Tübingen: J. C. B. Mohr [Paul Siebeck], 1981).

35. Carl Holsten's 1861 essay, "Die Christusvision des Paulus," was reprinted in *Zum Evangelium des Paulus und Petrus* (Rostock: Stiller'sche Hofbuchhandlung, 1868), 65–114. It was prefaced by a critique of Beyschlag, whose work, critical of Holsten, had appeared in 1864.

the heavenly Son of God, in a spiritual luminous body. Holsten claimed that because visionary experiences occur independently of the will, their recipient construes them as objective, though actually they are visualized thoughts. In Paul's case, everything turned on the fact that the Christians he persecuted claimed that the crucified Jesus was the Messiah. This contradiction between the Christian claims and Paul's convictions generated the anxiety that he might be wrong, a dilemma resolved by the vision. Willibald Beyschlag[36] rejected this interpretation, contending instead that Paul, like Luther, was driven by a sense of failure as described in Romans 7. Therefore, Paul's conversion was not the result of wrestling with a theological problem (Jesus' messiahship), nor did it rest on self-deception (i.e., he only thought he saw Jesus); it was a miraculous event. Otto Pfleiderer,[37] in turn, rejected Beyschlag and built on Holsten's foundations, contending that any psychological explanation must expose the root of Paul's distinctive message: the failure of the law and the alternate salvation in Christ. As a Jew, Paul might have been convinced of *his* failure but not of the law's. Holsten therefore had rightly seen the offense of the cross. Even before Paul became a Christian, he had seen, more clearly than the apostles, the "essential incompatibility of faith in the crucified Messiah and the old religion of the law." The inevitable logic of the Christian claims about Jesus contended with Paul's feelings until the decision of the mind prevailed, and took the form of a "sentient experience" (i.e., the vision), because Paul could not have contemplated seriously the possibility of Jesus' resurrection without forming an image of him. By regarding Paul's theology as a verbalized precipitate of inner experience, Pfleiderer derived virtually the whole of Paul's thought from his conversion.

The main difficulty with this debate is that it interpreted Paul in light of the visions reported only in Acts, which it accounted for psychologically by positing an inner conflict about which Paul himself says nothing at all—unless Romans 7 reports the tormented soul of the persecutor. But Werner Kümmel's dissertation[38] convinced most scholars, at least in Germany, that

36. Willibald Beyschlag's "Die Bekehrung des Ap. Paulus" appeared in *Studien u. Kritiken* in 1864. To Holsten's response of 1868 (see n. 32), Beyschlag replied with "Die Visionshypothese in ihrer neusten Begründung," *Studien u. Kritiken*, 1871. He summarized the issues in *New Testament Theology* (Edinburgh: T. & T. Clark, 1899), vol. 2.

37. Otto Pfleiderer, *Paulinism: A Contribution to the History of Primitive Christian Theology* (London: Williams & Norgate, 1891), vol. 1.

38. Werner G. Kümmel, *Römer 7 und die Bekehrung des Paulus* (Leipzig: J.C. Hinrichs, 1928). For a brief overview of the discussion, see Beda Rigaux, *The Letters of St. Paul* (Chicago: Franciscan Herald Press, 1968), 40–67.

this famous chapter could not be used to reconstruct the agony in the soul of the pre-Christian Paul because its apparent autobiographical statements actually rely on the first-person singular to make vivid an analysis of the pre-Christian human condition under the law as seen retrospectively through the prism of its solution in Christ; they do not report how Paul himself had agonized over the law.

No one has made Paul's conversion more significant for his theology than Kim,[39] who draws far-reaching conclusions from a synthesis of Acts and Paul. Like many others, Kim identifies those whom Paul persecuted as the Hellenistic Jewish Christians, who saw the validity of the temple and the ritual parts of the law abrogated because the Messiah had been crucified. Rejecting Bultmann's view that the core of Paul's conversion was a transformed self-understanding, Kim argues that Paul's vision revealed "the mystery of Christ"—Christ as the embodiment of God's plan of salvation, which in turn unified both the Pauline already-not yet dialectic of salvation and the necessity of the gentile mission before the salvation of the Jews (as Rom. 11:25 implies). In addition, the vision provided the basis of Paul's pre-existence Christology because he saw Christ as the image of God and as the Son of God, which led him to "conceive of Christ in terms of the personified . . . Wisdom of God (together with his realization at that time that Christ had superseded the Torah) on the one hand, and in terms of Adam, on the other" (267). All this corresponds to Jesus' self-designation as Son of Man. Moreover, the conversion revealed that God justifies the ungodly, namely, Paul himself. In fact, the major themes of Pauline soteriology are also traceable to the Damascus road—justification, reconciliation, and new creation. In short, "Paul's gospel and apostleship are grounded solely in the Christophany on the Damascus road" (267–68). Kim's case would be far more persuasive if he could show how he knows what Paul "saw." Moreover, he confuses a logical consonance between Paul's theology and his conversion with a genetic relation in which the latter produces the former. The overall result is that by claiming so much Kim has actually exposed how little one can show that the conversion experience accounts for the theology.

In retrospect, it must be admitted that the attempts to account for Paul's theology, whether by emphasizing its polemical character in response to opponents or by focusing on its personal quality because of his unique history and experience, have not fulfilled their promises, despite prodigious

39. See n. 34.

effort and impressive learning. At every point, the texts available impose
severe limits on what can be shown. Instead of marking clearly and
respecting consistently the boundaries of what is knowable, Pauline
scholarship frequently substituted inference for evidence, thereby forfeiting
self-criticism. Moreover, if one grants that Paul was "an original" who
burst on the scene with unusual energy, relentless zeal, and enormous
power of theological penetration, one should not expect to "explain" or
"account for" him any more than one does for any original mind. Can one
account for Bach?

Understanding Paul's Thought as Theology

The second persistent question concerns the nature of Paul's theology;
more precisely, the attempts to grasp his thought as theology, as a coherent
construal of God, Christ, and the human condition and its destiny. This
mode of inquiry does not abandon the historical mode; it is constantly
informed by it. But it does look for different things: instead of genetic relationships, influences, and consequences, it is concerned with the coherence
of the whole and with its constitutive element. These two concerns now
need attention.

Given the nature of the Pauline corpus, it is not surprising that from time
to time scholars have asked whether Paul was a *coherent thinker.* To understand Paul's thought as theology one must first assemble the pieces into as
coherent a whole as possible, giving each element its proper weight. J.
Louis Martyn saw that the problem is

> the way in which one moves from the mass of data before us in seven situational
> and highly variegated letters to the presentation of something that is recogniza-
> ble as a coherent structure of thought. Most of us are not satisfied to speak
> indefinitely of the thoughts of Paul, but the rub comes when we ask exactly
> how we go about avoiding that.[40]

What one takes to be the apostle's "coherent structure of thought" cus-
tomarily reveals itself in the way the material is presented. It has not been
unusual to present it in categories derived from the loci of classical Christian theology.[41] Because this approach assumes that what gives Paul's theol-

40. J. Louis Martyn, in a review of Beker's *Paul the Apostle* in *Word and World* (1982),
194–95.
41. See, e.g., George B. Stevens, *The Pauline Theology: A Study of the Origin and Correla-
tion of the Doctrinal Teachings of the Apostle Paul* (1892; New York: Charles Scribner's Sons,
1898); Fernand Prat, *The Theology of St. Paul* (London: Burns, Oates & Washbourne, 1927),
vol. 2.

ogy its coherence is congruent with the structure of systematic theology, Paul's ideas are collected from the letters and ordered according to the structure of the *ordo salutis* (plan of salvation), with anthropology (the human condition) sometimes replacing "creation" as the starting point and with eschatology consistently discussed last. Although this procedure has been criticized repeatedly, it persists until recent times, as the books by D. E. H. Whiteley and Herman Ridderbos show.[42] Even though the result makes it easy to learn "what Paul says about . . . , " it obscures Paul's own coherences. Above all, by making eschatology the last chapter, it transforms the locomotive which pulled Paul's train of thought into the caboose.

A quite opposite procedure reflects the conclusion that Paul's thought actually lacked coherence. No one argued this more rigorously than Hermann Lüdemann,[43] whose monograph remains one of the most brilliant studies between Baur and Bultmann, though few accept his conclusions completely. Lüdemann analyzed Paul's most sustained theological discussion, Romans. In chapters 5-8 he found that salvation consists of the destruction of the flesh and the liberation of the spirit through participation in Christ and the bestowal of the Spirit. From these chapters, he argued, Christ's atoning death, justification, and the centrality of faith are absent. These, however, are central in Romans 1—4. Point by point, Lüdemann contrasted the two soteriologies that Paul had juxtaposed. Galatians, he argued, agrees with Romans 1—4, but Corinthians with Romans 5—8. Ever since, scholars have wrestled with the relation between these two views of salvation, the participatory and the juridical (based on the problem of the law).

Lüdemann's most influential follower was Schweitzer, as the following quotation shows:

> Thus in Paul's writings there are two independent conceptions of the forgiveness of sins. According to the one, God forgives in consequence of the atoning death of Jesus; according to the other, He forgives, because through the dying and rising with Christ He has caused the flesh and sin to be abolished together, so that those who have died and risen with Christ are, in the eyes of God, sin-

42. D. E. H. Whiteley, *The Theology of St. Paul* (Philadelphia: Fortress Press, 1966); Herman Ridderbos, *Paul: An Outline of His Theology* (Grand Rapids: Wm. B. Eerdmans Co., 1975). Half a century earlier, Schweitzer had identified the flaws in this approach; see *Paul and His Interpreters*, 33.

43. Hermann Lüdemann, *Die Anthropologie des Apostels Paulus und ihre Stellung innerhalb seiner Heilslehre* (Kiel: Universitäts Buchhandlung, 1872).

less beings. The former of these doctrines is traditional, the latter is peculiar to Paul. . . . There is no argument against the validity of the Law to be derived directly from the atoning death of Jesus. [Contrast the construal of Paul's conversion, noted above.] All that can be done therefore is to bring the doctrine of freedom from the Law into close connection with the doctrine of the atoning death of Jesus by means of logical ingenuities.[44]

Schweitzer therefore concludes that justification by faith is not the heart of Paul's theology but a "subsidiary crater" within the main one, participation in Christ.[45] "All the blessings of redemption . . . flow from being-in-Christ and from this only."[46]

The extended quotation shows that despite the fact that Schweitzer praised Paul because he "vindicated for all time rights of thought in Christianity," and despite the fact that he claimed that " 'being-in-Christ' is the prime enigma in Paul's teaching; once grasped it gives the clue to the whole,"[47] he found a basic incoherence in the apostle's theology. How does he account for this? Because Paul's rhetoric compelled him to contrast doing the Law with faith, and because in defending justification by faith he was forced to rely on the only two biblical passages he could find that supported his case (Gen. 15:6; Hab. 2:4). Paul was unaware of his faulty logic, and it did not matter to him "that there is no logical route from the righteousness by faith to a theory of ethics."[48] One has the impression that for Schweitzer, the flaw in coherence is not serious because Paulinism is "nothing else than an eschatological mysticism, expressing itself by the aid of the Greek religious terminology."[49]

Other scholars have dealt with the diversity and coherence in Paul by claiming that his thought developed,[50] some focusing on his anthropology and ethics, some on his view of the law, but most on his eschatology. It is not clear, however, that our sources permit one to speak of development, since all the genuine letters (including their antecedent letters) were written within one decade. Moreover, it is one thing to note differences elicited by changed circumstances, another to construe the differences as "development."

44. Schweitzer, *The Mysticism of Paul the Apostle* (London: Adam & Charles Black, 1931), 223–24.
45. Ibid., 225.
46. Ibid., 206.
47. Ibid., 376, 3 resp.
48. Ibid., 225.
49. Schweitzer, *Paul and His Interpreters*, 241.
50. For a convenient, judicious survey of the more recent discussion, see Victor Paul Furnish, "Development in Paul's Thought," *Journal of the American Academy of Religion* 38 (1970): 289–303.

The other major concern of the attempts to understand Paul's thought as theology, as a "coherent structure of thought," is the quest for its constitutive factor. It is not enough to identify it as his Christology or soteriology, for that would be as true of the Fourth Gospel or the Letter to the Hebrews as it is of Paul. The constitutive factor, then, is that ingredient, or that "grammar," which gives Paul's "thoughts" their determinative structure and character. Generally speaking, the focus has oscillated between an anthropocentric and a theocentric reading of Paul's theology, though it would be foolish to force the whole history of interpretation into one of two boxes.

The anthropocentric focus begins with F. C. Baur's book on Paul (see note 2), where the real subject matter of Paul's theology is the principle of Christian consciousness, which for Baur was the identity of the subjective human spirit with the objective Spirit of God. This principle, being "essentially identical with the person of Christ," is absolute, and asserts itself "by overcoming all that conflicts with its supremacy" (123). Its absoluteness, moreover, makes Paul conscious of "the essential difference of the spirit from the flesh, of freedom from everything by which man is only outwardly affected, of the reconciliation of man with God, and of man's union with God. . . . The Christian knows himself to be identical with the Spirit of God" (126).

How does this come about in our own consciousness? By allowing Christ, in whom the human and divine Spirit are identical, to become the governing principle of our own consciousness:

> What Christ is to us objectively, as the object of our consciousness . . . he is to become to us subjectively; that which is now objective is to become identical with ourselves by [our] being changed into the same image. . . . This cannot but be the case, since the transformation proceeds from the Lord, whose whole essence is Spirit. (132)

From the standpoint of this consciousness of identity with the absolute Spirit, the Christian looks at the world in an entirely different way.

"Wisdom and folly change places" but to the person who lives only by the finite, who has not allowed himself/herself to be governed by the absolute, the absolute does not exist and is regarded as folly. The person who "occupies the absolute standpoint possesses in it the absolute standard for everything that is merely relative. . . . In all this we have the explanation which the Apostle himself has given us of the principle of his Christian consciousness" (133).

Paul arrived at this consciousness by being reconciled with God; the negative side of the experience entails discerning both the capacity of the law and the power of the flesh; its positive meaning is justification by faith.

> He who is justified by faith must first of all believe that this is so, and since the objective truth of justification consists in this, that what the justified person is to his own consciousness, he is also in the consciousness of God . . . it must be a fact in the consciousness of God that he who is himself unjust, is yet just. (158)

In other words, for Baur consciousness of the identity of the human and divine Spirit is the constitutive center in Paul's theology, because this consciousness of reality = reconciliation = justification by faith. (On this basis, there is no ground for a cleavage between the juridical and the participatory views of salvation.) So completely does this (soteriological) analysis of the consciousness of identity dominate Baur's exposition that the apostle's "thoughts" about God, Christ, angels, demons, and so forth, are relegated to the penultimate chapter, virtually an appendix.

Despite the strangeness of this language of German philosophy of identity, Baur's remains one of the most penetrating, logically developed and architectonically balanced, and beautifully written construal of Paul's theology until today. In substance, though not in style, only Bultmann's presentation of Paul is in the same league, though relying on a philosophy virtually the opposite of Baur's.

Bultmann's interpretation of Paul is the high-water mark of the anthropocentric reading of the Apostle. Bultmann finds the fact that Paul does not write paragraphs about God's being or nature (scarcely to be expected, given the nature of the letters) to be congenial with the existentialist passion to overcome "objectivism," and so he points out that Paul's theology deals with God only "as He is significant for man, for man's responsibility, and man's salvation." Consequently, Paul's theology is really anthropology, and his "Christology is simultaneously soteriology." In other words, "Paul's theology can best be treated as his doctrine of man; first, man prior to revelation of faith, and second of man under faith, for in this way the anthropological and soteriological orientation . . . is brought out."[51]

The presentation of Paul's theology carries this out consistently. Bultmann begins by analyzing the constituent elements of the self as created, but swiftly moves to the actualities in which the self finds itself: flesh and

---

51. Bultmann, *Theology of the New Testament*, I:191.

sin, sin and death, world, law, and so forth. This is nothing other than an analysis of the fallen *Mensch,* in existentialist terms. When Bultmann turns to "Man under Faith," he discusses the Righteousness of God, Grace as Event (Christology, ecclesiology, sacraments), and Faith and Freedom (Spirit, ethics, and eschatology in an existentialist idiom).

By viewing Paul's whole theology through the anthropological prism, however, Bultmann can (must?) virtually ignore the theme of "Israel," and bypass Romans 9—11. Likewise, by reading Paul as emphasizing the presence of salvation, he must relegate apocalyptic to the margin, as a more or less Jewish holdover from earlier Christianity: Paul's expectation of the end of the old world at the coming of Christ "can only be the confirmation of the eschatological occurrence that has now already begun." Inevitably, the redemption of the world, tersely formulated in Rom. 8:18–25, does not receive its due. He cites this passage only to make two points: first, that "Gnostic mythology lies behind the allusion to the fall of creation in Rom. 8:20ff."; second, to recast also this into existentialist language:

> Creation becomes a destructive power whenever man decides in favor of it instead of for God. . . . Hence it owes to man himself such independence as it has toward God. . . . Paul's conception of the creation, as well as of the Creator, depends upon what it means for man's existence. (1:230–31)

Clearly, Bultmann's discussion of Paul reflects his view that the task of theology is to explicate the self-understanding of faith as response to the Word of God (see above); theology presents "not the object of faith [God, Christ, etc.] but faith itself in its own self-interpretation" (2:239).

Since in Bultmann's reading of Paul the temporal and cosmic horizons of apocalyptic were minimalized while an individual-centered anthropology was the focus, it is not surprising that the shift to a theocentric reading would emphasize apocalyptic as well. Both are manifest in Käsemann's critique of his former teacher.

The new direction, which was consummated in Käsemann's commentary on Romans, had been foreshadowed by a series of articles, beginning with "Sentences of Holy Law" (1954)[52]—statements like "If anyone destroys God's temple [the body], God will destroy him" (1 Cor. 3:17), which are found not only in Paul but also in sayings attributed to Jesus (e.g., Mark 8:38). The force of his analysis of these statements was formulated aptly six years later when Käsemann explicitly turned to early Christian apocalyptic:

52. Ernst Käsemann, "Sentences of Holy Law in the New Testament," in *New Testament Questions of Today* (Philadelphia: Fortress Press, 1969), 66–81.

Nowhere is there a clearer expression [than in these "Sentences"] of the view-point which reckons with the imminent invasion of the Parousia, professing to know the criteria with which the universal Judge operates and deriving this knowledge from its own inspiration of the Spirit.[53]

According to Käsemann, early Christianity generally was characterized by *Enthusiasmus*—a heady celebration of the presence of salvation, quite similar to Bousset's description of the *Kyrios*-cult. In other words, whereas Bousset had assigned apocalyptic to earliest Jerusalem Christianity and *Enthusiasmus* (a word he did not use) to later Hellenistic Christianity, Käsemann found both in Jerusalem, where Jewish Christianity saw "in the possession of the Spirit the pledge of the imminent Parousia and the ambassadorial authority for its mission" (92). The "Sentences of Holy Law," then, are evidence that Spirit-generated *Enthusiasmus* and apocalyptic were intertwined and reinforced each other from the outset. Moreover, this fusion was something new, because according to Käsemann Jesus himself "did not bear a fundamentally apocalyptic stamp but proclaimed the immediacy of the God who was near at hand" (101). In other words, whereas William Wrede had seen Paul as the "second founder of Christianity," Käsemann saw a new beginning in earliest Christianity because one must "recognize in post-Easter apocalyptic a new theological start." Therefore, "apocalyptic was the mother of all Christian theology" (102).

Käsemann made another decisive move when he concluded that important as the theme of divine retribution was in the "Sentences," the heart of apocalyptic lies elsewhere—in "the accession to the throne of heaven by God and by his Christ . . . an event which can also be characterized as proof of the righteousness of God" (105). With this, he redefined the theological content of apocalyptic: it expressed God's sovereign action in reclaiming all creation from rebellion. Now came the sentence that set the agenda for the future:

But exactly the same thing seems to me to be happening in the Pauline doctrine of God's righteousness and our justification which I therefore derive, so far as the history of religion is concerned, from apocalyptic. This can have been the only reason why primitive Christian parenesis [exhortation] was primarily grounded in apocalyptic.

A year later, Käsemann published his pivotal study of the righteousness of God in Paul.[54] In a time of massive monographs and multivolume com-

53. Ernst Käsemann, " 'The Righteousness of God' in Paul," in *New Testament Questions of Today*, 168–82.
54. Ibid.

mentaries on a single book, Käsemann redirected the study of Paul with an essay of a mere fourteen pages. Now the break with the Bultmannian interpretation of Paul was complete. Käsemann not only anchored Paul's view of God's righteousness in apocalyptic, but redefined it: while agreeing that in Phil. 3:9 the phrase does refer to God's gift to the believer, he also insisted that in Rom. 3:25–26 it refers to God's own righteousness. Moreover, he appealed to the Old Testament and the Dead Sea Scrolls to argue that God's righteousness refers to God's saving power.

Thus God's righteousness is God's sovereignty over the world, revealing itself eschatologically in Jesus. . . . It is the rightful power with which God makes his cause to triumph in the world which has fallen away from him and which yet, as creation, is his inviolable possession. (108)

Accordingly, God's righteousness (and justification) does not refer primarily to God's gift to the believer, nor is it to be construed as part of Paul's anthropology. Thus Käsemann argued that in Paul's theology God could be spoken of, and must be spoken of, in ways far broader than God's significance for the believing self.

In responding to the sharp dissent his essays provoked, Käsemann went on to say that whereas earliest Jewish Christianity had blended *Enthusiasmus* and apocalyptic, on Hellenistic soil, and especially in Corinth, there developed an *Enthusiasmus* that lacked a clear future expectation—more or less as Bousset described. As a result, whereas the earlier history of religion emphasis had seen Paul as the propagator and purifier of this Hellenistic Christianity, Käsemann saw Paul as waging in Corinth an anti-Enthusiast battle under the banner of apocalyptic. In doing so, Paul did not repudiate "present eschatology" outright, but built into it an "eschatological reservation" and emphasized that Christ's present lordship is destined to end (1 Cor. 15:20–28). "No perspective could be more apocalyptic."[55]

The shift to a theocentric reading of Paul is marked also in the work of J. Christiaan Beker,[56] though his agenda differs from Käsemann's. In order to do justice to both the coherent center of Paul's thought and to each letter's contingency on particular circumstances (and the resultant diversity in Paul's statements), Beker emphasizes the hermeneutical character of the apostle's theology. "His hermeneutic consists in the constant interaction

55. Ernst Käsemann, "On the Subject of Primitive Christian Apocalyptic," in *New Testament Questions of Today*, 132–33.
56. J. Christiaan Beker, *Paul the Apostle* (Philadelphia: Fortress Press, 1980).

between the coherent center of the gospel and its contingent interpretation"
(11). This center is

> a Christian apocalyptic structure of thought—derived from a constitutive
> primordial experience [Paul's conversion/call] and delineating the Christ-event
> in its meaning for the apocalyptic consummation of history, that is, in its mean-
> ing for the triumph of God. (16)

Despite an emphasis on apocalyptic, Beker differentiates his interpretation
from both Schweitzer and Käsemann. He does so by distinguishing the primary language (or "deep structure") from the secondary ("surface structure"); the former is the apocalyptic meaning of Christ, while the
latter—the contingent—is the particular linguistic expression, like justification and participation in Christ. This approach differentiates him from
Schweitzer who regarded the "being-in-Christ" as the constitutive center,
and from Käsemann as well, who, by grounding justification in apocalyptic, made justification the determinative content. By regarding justification
as the contingent symbol, Beker is not obligated, as is Käsemann, to show
how it percolates through Paul's thought as a whole. In other words,
apocalyptic, having been relieved of its mystical construal on the one side
and distinguished from its contingent construal as justification on the other,
is exposed as a self-consistent coherent center: the theme of God's impending triumph begun in the event of Christ. Beker's task, then, is to show how
this constitutive center is interpreted into the series of contingent expressions found in the letters.

Because Beker thinks that "Paul was an apocalyptist during his Pharisaic
career" (143), he must account for the absence of many apocalyptic ideas
from the letters; he does so by calling to witness Paul's conversion/call,
arguing also that "the reduction of apocalyptic terminology and the
absence of apocalyptic speculation signifies that the Christ-event has
strongly modified the dualistic structure of normal apocalyptic thought"
(145). Beker's chapter on Christ's resurrection, seen against the horizon of
real futuristic apocalyptic theology, which Paul brought to bear on the
Corinthian crisis (as Käsemann also claimed), is the high point of the book.
Moreover, Beker's discussion of the cross does what Schweitzer said could
not be done (link atonement and justification): "The death of Christ signifies the great reversal, because the judgment of the Torah on Christ [Gal.
3:13] becomes instead the judgment of God in Christ on the Torah" (186).
Not only did Paul interpret the cross apocalyptically (e.g., it defeats the
invisible spiritual powers), but he also interpreted its saving effects dialecti-
cally, not sequentially as in apocalyptic. That is, "life is not just life after

death but also life in the midst of death"—an insight that Beker suggests may be original with Paul (187). Like Käsemann, Beker regards Paul's apocalyptic perspective as not only profound but as profoundly valid also for our own time.

Instead of a Conclusion

It would be arrogant to write a Conclusion because the critical study of Paul's theology continues (as does the study of the study of Paul); besides, this essay is but a sketch from which both important scholars and significant issues have been omitted. Two persistent issues might well have been included—Paul's relation to the Jesus-traditions and Paul's ethics. Including them, however, would have expanded the essay unduly. Moreover, important elements in Jesus-Paul debate were summarized on pages 38–43. In any case, it is more appropriate to end this essay by stating succinctly some observations about the study of Paul as a whole.   *good on letters*

First, although few indeed are the questions that are settled, today it is   ✓ generally accepted that the discussion of Paul's thought must proceed on the basis of the seven uncontested letters (Romans, 1 and 2 Corinthians, Galatians, Philippians, 1 Thessalonians, Philemon). Scholars who regard also Ephesians, Colossians, and 2 Thessalonians as genuine (few scholars regard the Pastorals as genuine) recognize that the more their construal of Paul's thought depends on one or more of these three, the less persuasive it is to their peers who regard them as deutero-Pauline. Therefore the former too base their understanding of Paul on the seven letters. As a corollary, it is commonly recognized that the authoritativeness of a letter for religious and theological purposes does not depend on whether Paul himself was its author.

Second, there is growing recognition that Paul's letters were edited and   ?2 compiled into the letters we have, although scholars have reached no real consensus about the literary integrity of all the letters. The probability that at least 2 Corinthians and Philippians, and possibly Romans and 1 Corinthians as well, are compilations produces an unexpected result: although from the standpoint of genuineness, the canonical corpus of thirteen letters has been reduced to seven, from the standpoint of literary integrity the number of letters Paul actually wrote has increased. Few agree, however, with Schmithals, who claims to have discovered twenty-five letters or letter fragments in the uncontested seven.[57] In any case, if the letters have been

57. Walter Schmithals, *Die Briefe des Paulus in ihrer ursprünglichen Form* (Zürich: Theologischer Verlag, 1984).

compiled, the task of studying Paul's thought is both simplified and made more complex; simplified because the internal differences (which led to the conclusion that a given letter is composite) need no longer be harmonized because they reflect Paul's responses to changed circumstances, more complex because now one must reconstruct more situations to account for his expanded correspondence.

Moreover, one must also reckon with the possibility that the editor, whose identity is wholly unknown, also omitted parts of the letters. Given the texts at hand, there is no way to prove this.[58] Still, in reconstructing Paul's ministry and thought scholars should have reckoned more seriously with this possibility than they have; doing so might have made some of their arguments less self-assured. Indeed, the task is rather like assembling a jigsaw puzzle from which an uncertain number of pieces may be missing, and to which pieces from other puzzles (interpolations) might have been added as well.

Third, from another angle, scholars have indeed become aware of how complex a task it is to reconstruct Paul's thought and its place in early Christianity. This awareness results in the remarkable increase in the amount of material that must now be considered, each with its own historical-critical problems. Indeed, one might well write the history of research in Christian origins in terms of the impact of successive discoveries and publication of newly found texts, both Christian (e.g., Gospel of Peter, Didache, Nag Hammadi library) and non-Christian (e.g., the Mandaean literature, Dead Sea Scrolls). As a result, it has become ever more evident that the world in which Paul was at home was far more kaleidoscopic, and much more resistant to facile generalizations, than had been thought. Unfortunately, the relentless drift toward ever narrower specialization has made it more difficult for students of early Christianity to master the whole range of material.

Fourth, by and large, scholars who sought to provide a historical-critical explanation of Paul and his theology have not been sufficiently self-critical about their historiography. Bultmann is one of the few who pondered what is entailed in writing history. Such reflection is especially important when the reconstructed web of historical relationships is expected to provide the explanatory context for a figure like Paul. Sustained reflection on the com-

---

58. The text in Romans is not really an exception because although there is evidence that this letter circulated in three forms—one with 14 chapters, one with 15, and the present one with 16 chapters—the shorter forms are later abbreviations of the 16-chapter letter, not its antecedents.

plexity of the historical task, or on the nature of historical explanation and its vocabulary (e.g., cause, influence, derivation, consequence), might have exposed some of the unclaimed freight that accompanied the use of the standard vocabulary of the discipline (e.g., Paul's "borrowing") and which frequently skews the discussion in subtle and unnoticed ways. Moreover, other questions need to be raised, such as: Is "conversion" really the appropriate word for Paul's coming to faith in Christ?[59] What distortions are introduced by using certain terms anachronistically, such as "Christianity" or "theology"? What value judgments are smuggled into all talk of Paul's "development"? At what points have scholars created unnecessary problems by labeling something as "gnostic" or "apocalyptic"? In short, a self-critical history of research would be a most welcome addition to the literature.

Fifth, similar absence of self-criticism has marked also the attempts to determine Paul's relation to early Christianity, including his use of traditions and traditional concepts. Nonetheless, it must be emphasized that tradition- and redaction-critical analysis have led to a much more careful reading of the texts, a clear gain for exegesis generally. Differences in style, vocabulary, and conceptuality must be identified precisely if one is to recover traditions from texts. What has been wanting, however, is a coherent, historically plausible understanding of how tradition functioned in antiquity, and in particular in early Christianity. As a result, often it has been assumed that Paul's adaptations of the traditions were really his theologically motivated "corrections" rather than clarifications, as he might have regarded them.

To a large extent, scholars may have been victimized by the procedures of the redaction-critical method itself. In order to make a credible case for Paul's use of tradition, one emphasizes the differences between the alleged tradition and Paul's own mode of expression or thought. This, in turn, raises the question of why he would have used something he found faulty. The answer commonly given is that he did so in order to "correct" it. One cannot avoid wondering, however, whether this is how tradition functioned, and whether this is how Paul understood his own relation to it. Important as the redaction-critical analysis has been in showing the extent to which Paul was indebted to the growing common stock of early Christian traditions, it still leaves the impression that he was something of a loner who insisted that his own distinctive accents must always be asserted—rather

---

59. Krister Stendahl rightly objected to the use of this term for Paul's experience. *Paul Among Jews and Gentiles* (Philadelphia: Fortress Press, 1976), 7-13.

like an academic in a seminar. It would be instructive to discern the degree to which the history of philosophy model, which emphasizes the distinctive moves made vis-à-vis one's own predecessor—Plato and Socrates, Aristotle and Plato, Marx and Hegel, and so forth—has affected the assumptions that shaped the treatment of Paul and his predecessors.

Finally, then, what can be said about the course that the historical-critical study of Paul has taken? Despite the limitations this essay has exposed, the contribution to the understanding of Paul and his theology has been decisive and it is enduring. It is also essential, for its efforts keep reminding us that the apostle's theology is not a disembodied set of ideas. Rather, he and his thought were deeply rooted in a particular time and place, and he addressed readers who also were at home in a culture in many ways different from our own, yet one that faced certain issues endemic to the human condition. It is part of the genius of the historical-critical method that it has the capacity to make this concrete, even if in a limited way, and that it can be self-correcting as well. The newer literary/structuralist and sociological/anthropological approaches are supplementing it, but they will not replace it. Nor should they, for it is the historical-critical method that keeps us in touch with the unrepeatable reality of the past, and so reminds us of our own contingency as well as Paul's.[60]

---

60. See also my "Will the Historical-Critical Method Survive? Some Observations," in *Orientation by Disorientation*, Beardslee Festschrift, ed. Richard A. Spencer (Pittsburgh: Pickwick Press, 1980), 115-27.

SCRIPTURE INDEX